कणादटिप्पन्या समलङ्कृते
गङ्गेशाचार्यस्य
पक्षताचिन्तामणिः एवं सामान्यनिरुक्तिः

Pakṣtācintāmaṇi and Sāmānyanirukti

of Gaṅgeśa

with Kaṇādaṭippani

Prakashika Series
No. 4

General Editor
Dipti S. Tripathi

कणादटिप्पन्या समलङ्कृते गङ्गेशाचार्यस्य पक्षताचिन्तामणिः एवं सामान्यनिरुक्तिः

आङ्गलभाषानुवादेन संवलितं मूलम्

सम्पादक

सुबुद्धि चरण गोस्वामी

राष्ट्रीय पाण्डुलिपि मिशन

नई दिल्ली

तथा

देव पब्लिशर्स एण्ड डिस्ट्रीब्यूटर्स

प्रकाशक :

राष्ट्रीय पाण्डुलिपि मिशन

11, मानसिंह रोड,
नई दिल्ली-110 001

दूरभाष: 2338 3894; फैक्स: 2307 3387

e-mail: directornamami@nic.in
website: www.namami.nic.in

सह-प्रकाशक :

देव पब्लिशर्स एण्ड डिस्ट्रीब्यूटर्स

द्वितीय तल, प्रकाशदीप बिल्डिंग,
22, दिल्ली मैडिकल एसोसिएशन रोड
नई दिल्ली-110002

दूरभाष: 4357 2647

e-mail: devbooks@hotmail.com
website: www.devbooks.co.in

ISBN 978-93-80829-02-9 (Series)
ISBN 978-93-80829-14-2 (Vol. IV)
प्रथम संस्करण: 2013

मूल्य: ₹ 225.00

Pakṣtācintāmaṇi and Sāmānyanirukti of Gaṅgeśa with Kaṇādaṭippani

(Text and English Translation)

Critically edited by
Subuddhi Charan Goswami

राष्ट्रीय पाण्डुलिपि मिशन
॥ विज्ञानमुपास्व ॥
National Mission for Manuscripts
Dev Publishers & Distributors

Published by:
National Mission for Manuscripts
Indira Gandhi National Centre for the Arts
11 Man Singh Road
New Delhi 110 001
Phone: 91 11 2307 3387
e-mail: directornamami@nic.in
website: www.namami.nic.in

and Co-published by:
Dev Publishers & Distributors
2nd Floor, Prakash Deep,
22, Delhi Medical Association Road,
Darya Ganj,
New Delhi-110002
Phone: 91 114357 2647
e-mail: devbooks@hotmail.com
website: www.devbooks.co.in

ISBN 978-93-80829-02-9 (Series)
ISBN 978-93-80829-14-2 (Vol. IV)
First published 2013

Contents

Key to Transliteration

VOWELS

अ a	आ ā	इ i	ई ī	उ u	ऊ ū
(but)	(palm)	(it)	(beet)	(put)	(pool)
ऋ ṛ	ए e	ऐ ai	ओ o	औ au	
(rhythm)	(play)	(air)	(toe)	(loud)	

CONSONANTS

Guttural	क ka	ख* kha	ग ga	घ gha	ङ ṅa
	(skate)	(blockhead)	(gate)	(ghost)	(sing)
Palatal	च ca	छ cha	ज ja	झ jha	ञ ña
	(chunk)	(catchhim)	(john)	(hedgehog)	(bunch)
Cerebral	ट ṭa	ठ* ṭha	ड/ड़ ḍa	ढ*/ढ़ ḍha	ण* ṇa
	(start)	(anthill)	(dart)	(godhead)	(under)
Dental	त ta	थ tha	द da	ध dha	न na
	(path)	(thunder)	(that)	(breathe)	(numb)
Labial	प pa	फ* pha	ब ba	भ bha	म ma
	(spin)	(philosophy)	(bin)	(abhor)	(much)
Semi-vowels	य ya	र ra	ल la	व va	
	(young)	(drama)	(luck)	(vile)	
Sibilants	श śa	ष ṣa	स sa	ह ha	
	(shove)	(bushel)	(so)	(hum)	
Others	क्ष kṣa	त्र tra	ज्ञ jña	ळ* l	ॠ* ṝ
	(*kṣātriya*)	(*triśūla*)	(*jñānī*)	(play)	

अं (—) *ṁ* or *ṃ amusūra* (nasalisation of preceding vowel) like *saṁskṛti/or soṃskṛti*

अः *visarga* = *ḥ* (aspiration of preceding vowel like (*prātaḥ*)

ऽ *Avagraha* consonant #' consonant (like-*imé vasthitā*)

Anusvāra at the end of a line is presented by m (म्) and not *ṁ*

*No exact English equivalents for these letters.

Foreword

Over the ages the six systems of Indian philosophy have been enriched by scholars in the respective system. Of these, there is a marked affinity between Sāṅkhya and Yoga and Nyāya and Vaiśeṣika. The Nyāya and Vaiśeṣika systems of philosophy depend heavily on validation of knowledge through evidence (pramāṇa). It is held that knowledge is acquired through pramāṇa only. In the old school of Nyāya which began with the Nyāyasūtra of Gautama four pramāṇas were established which are pratyakṣa, anumāna, upamāna and śabda. That is why in all the sixteen categories of Nyāya philosophy pramāṇa has been accorded the first position. A lot of discussion and exposition has taken place regarding the precision of pramāṇas in the texts of Nyāyaśāstra as also that of Vaiśeṣika. The systems of Vaiśeṣika and Nyāya fused together to create what is now known as Navya-Nyāya. It was given an authentic form by Gangeśa Upādhyāya of Mithila in the 14th century. His magnum opus is named Tattvacintāmaṇi. This text is based on the first category of Nyāyasūtra i.e. Pramāṇa.

The above text is divided into four parts according to four pramāṇas accepted by the Naiyāyikās. It acquired pre-eminent position amongst scholars which led to several commentaries and sub-commentaries being written. The Navya-Nyāya School originated in Mithila but flourished in Bengal and most of the acknowledged scholars of this school come from this region. Kaṇāda Tarkavagīśa is one such stalwart who is believed to have lived in the second half of the fifteenth century AD. He wrote extensively on Navya-Nyāya. Some were independent texts like Bhāṣāratnam and Tarkavādārthamañjarī. There is lack of unanimity regarding Apaśabadakhaṇḍanam. It is now believed to be the work of one Kanotka. Kaṇāda wrote a commentary on Gangeśa's anumāna (inference) section which is called Anumānacintāmaṇitippaṇī. The present text is only a portion of the tippaṇī on the whole of Anumāna Khaṇḍa.

Pakṣatā forms a major component of the process of inference

(anumāna). The three attributes of hetu-pakṣasattva, sapakṣasattva and vipakṣavyāvṛtisattva—integral to correct inference depend on the precise definition of pakṣatā. The present text of tippaṇī of Kaṇāda has been taken from a signle copy of the manuscript available at Bangiya Sahitya Parisad. The Mission will be obliged to scholars if they will provide us with information on any other copy available.

Sāmānyanirukti is the portion of Tattvacintāmaṇi giving the definition of Hetvābhāsa. Proper identification of Hetvābhāsa is equally, if not more, important than correct. Hetu, for inference to be irrefutable. Two copies of this portion of Tippaṇī were procured by the editor and edited with due diligence.

Dr. Subuddhi Charan Goswami has done a creditable work of presenting this text along with English translation which adds to its usefulness for scholars. He has also given in two appendices the relevant portions of the tikās of Raghunātha Śiromaṇi and Mathurānātha.

I do hope Dr. Goswami will someday be able to present the whole text of the tippaṇī to the scholarly world.

Dipti S. Tripathi
Director, NMM

Preface

(*Pakṣatā and Sāmānyanirukti*)

'vicintya dūrvādalavarṇaśobhā-pādaprafullotpalareṇuvāram/
tanoti yatnena Kaṇādanāmnā cintāmaṇiścintitagūḍhamartham//

The history of Indian philosophy which dates back to a hoary past of Vedic civilization has been gradually developed down the ages. The development was never monolithic, but multifold. A number of philosophical systems, sprang up along which *Nyāyavaiśeṣika* system occupies a special position. This system again gave birth to a significant school, which is known as '*Navya-Nyāya*' at the hand of Gaṅgeśa Upādhyāya by his monumental work 'Tattvacintāmaṇi'. Gaṅgeśa flourished in the 14th century AD in Mithila, but in later period his philosophy flooded Bengal by its overwhelming style of interpretation and language. For last six hundred years, the most significant and original contribution of Bengal in the academic world is *Navya-Nyāya,* apart from Grammar and *Smṛti* literature.

This 'Preface' neither contemplates to paint a comprehensive picture of the Bengal's contribution to *Navya-Nyāya.* Scholars can gather information from other sources i.e., in the books, depicting the history of Indian philosophy written by scholars both in English and Bengali.

But, as a matter of fact, we must reiterate that for last six hundred years, if Bengal had gifted anything substantial to the academic world, anything intrinsic, certainly it is the new system of Indian philosophy, better known as *Navya-Nyāya.* Based on the new system, propagated by 'Gaṅgeśa and his son Vardhamāna, tens of hundreds of texts, commentaries, sub-commentaries, annotations, have been composed; thousands of scholars spent their lives and brain to understand the logic, new terminology and a complete new style of Sanskrit language. Navadwipa once was recognized as the 'Oxford of East'. Benaras, the second home for the Bengali scholars, became the seat of learning. Dinesh Chandra Bhattacharya, in his stupendous work. *Bangalir*

Saraswata Avadan; 'Bange Navyanyaya Charcha' (published 1358 B.S., second edition 1414 B.S.), made a scientific effort through field-study to prepare a history of the *Navya-Nyāya* and the *Naiyāyikas* of Bengal, who resided in undivided Bengal and Beneras. Interested persons may get an idea from his book, what Bengal contributed for this special branch of knowledge. But unfortunately, the huge corpus of knowledge, due to its hard outer coverage in the form of cryptic language, is getting fast out of sight. About its peculiar language, even Gadādhara, the *Naiyāyika* of Bengal, sarcastically commented "*janeṣu jaḍacetasāṃ taruṇa eva karṇajvara"* (To the people who are not wellversed, it appears to them to be an acute ear-fever). The European Pandit Ward, who had a deep regard for *Navya-Nyāya* school and who commented—"*Indeed in philosophy, the Hindus have perhaps excelled both the Ancients and Moderns*", could feel it '*a system of wrangling and contention about names and terms*', Cowell, who learnt *Navya-Nyāya* from Mahesha Nyāyaratna, failed to understand the intrinsic logomachy of this system and commented, it is a fruitless effort of getting true knowledge at the end. It is, according to him, '*misdirected the zeal and useless the knowledge*', he understood—'*it's sole end is vicāra', (vitaṇḍā*). A.B. Keith does not differ much from Cowell, when he writes—"*a vast mass of perverted ingenuity worthy of the most flourishing days of medieval scholarsticism*" (*Indian Logic and Atomism,* p. 35). Even Iswarchandra Vidyasagar or Rabindra Nath Tagore, the best fruits of Indian Renaissance did not have a favourable outlook on *Navya-Nyāya.*

In spite of all odds, a lean and thin flow of teacher-taught tradition continued on *Navya-Nyāya* throughtout Bengal till 20th century AD. It is a matter of fact that thousands of manuscripts written on *Navya-Nyāya* have gone out of sight, the number of scholars in this field is fast decaying. In Bengal, Professor Ananta Lal Thakur may be the last stalwart in this field after Phani Bhusan Tarkavagish. Here lies the basic importance of editing such books.

Let us now come back to the main issue. *Tattvacintāmaṇi* by Gaṅgeśa, who is the chief architect of *Navya-Nyāya* System, is divided into four parts. *Pratyakṣa* (perception), *Anumiti* (inference), *Upamiti* (analogy) and *Śabda* (verbal testimony). *Pratyakṣa* portion is divided into 12 sub-sections, but the largest section is *Anumiti* in 17 sub-sections. *Upamiti* is comparatively small in size and *Śabda* section is again comprised of 16 sub-sections under different titles. Gaṅgeśa was born some 600 years back in Mithila and thenceforth the era of *Navya-Nyāya* begins. The largest corpus of *Navya-Nyāya* texts begins with Gaṅgeśa's, *Tattvacintāmaṇi.* The editor of this text Professor Subuddhi

Charan Goswami has given elaborate description about these sections and sub-sections in the Introduction.

Kaṇāda Tarkavagīśa may be regarded as one of the most prominent neo-logicians of this school who belonged probably to the 16th century AD. His birthplace was Khanakul-Krishnanagar of Bengal (See D.C. Bhattacharya, *Bange Navya-Nyāya Charcha,* pp. 108-11). He was the disciple of Janakinath Bhattacharya Chudamaṇi. Among his works, *Bhāṣāratna* has been edited by Kalipada Tarkacharya from Calcutta. But his chief work is a commentary on *Anumāna*-section of Gaṅgeśa Udādhyāya. The text is known as '*Anumānacintāmaṇiṭippanī* which is so far unpublished. The record of D.C. Bhattacharya (see p. 109fn.), shows that there are three copies of this text of which two copies are in the possession of Asiatic Society. The editor of this text, Professor Goswami, informs that in these two copies of the text '*pakṣatā*-section' is wanting. He discovered in the collections of 'Government Sanskrit College', Kolkata, prepared the text on the basis of a single copy of the manuscript. Aufrecht's *Catalogus Catalogorum* and *New Catalogus Catalogorum* (Madras), do not supply any extra information on this text. (Professor Goswami has given detail of the manuscript in his 'Indroduction'.

The present edition comprises two portions of *Anumāna-cintāmaṇiṭippanī* of Kaṇāḍa. The first part i.e. *pakṣatā* section is based on a single copy and the second part on *Anumāna* is on two aforesaid copies, preserved in Asiatic Society. The general definition of *Hetvābhāsa* of Gaṅgeśa goes by the title *Sāmānyanirukti* and thus the commentary of Kaṇāda is also known by the title *Sāmānyaniruktiṭippanī'*. The present text is the commentary on the definition of *Hetvābhāsa* of *Cintāmaṇi*. The editor has clarified the matter in his 'Editorial Note'. Thus it is a text of two parts clubbed within a single cover.

Regarding the editing part, we are grateful to the authorities of Government Sanskrit College, Kolkata and Asiatic Society, Kolkata, for giving copies of manuscripts. The present text has been designed as follows:

The original text of *Cintāmaṇi* of Gaṅgeśa has been placed first in bold letters followed by the commentary of *Kaṇādaṭippanī*. The *Tippanī* has been separated by passages, so that the original text of *Cintāmaṇi* of Gaṅgeśa can be better understood. The commentary has been translated into English, so that, it can be helpful for those, who find it difficult sometimes to read the original Sanskrit text. For *pakṣatā* section, as there was no second copy available, the editor had to take help of secondary sources for emendation and that has been recorded in end notes of *Pakṣatā*. But, for the *Sāmānyaniruktiṭippanī'*, the text has been constructed on the basis of two copies of manuscript. The Critical Apartus has been used for this purpose and variant readings are put in the lower part. The description of the manuscripts has been given by the editor himself in his editorial note separately for the two texts. Two Appendices are added on *Sāmānyanirukti* for better understanding of the original text of *Cintāmaṇi* and a comparative understanding of the commentators. Appendix I is of Raghunātha Śiromaṇi and Appendix II is of Mathurānātha (*Māthurī*). The total approach is contemplated for two distinct primal purposes. First of all, it is to bring out the unpublished text of Kaṇāda Tarkavāgīśa, which was so far unavailable to interested scholars. Secondly, the translation of the commentary and the commentaries of Raghunātha and Mathurānātha on the same topic have been incorporated so that the readers may enjoy the intellectual discourses of Bengal's neo-logicians on the topic.

The Department of Sanskrit, Rabindra Bharati University, Kolkata, undertook a major UGC Research Project DRS I (under SAP, UGC), on editing texts based on unpublished manuscripts on Indian Philosophy, Grammar and Literature, (2007-2012). It also focused on re-editing of rare texts. Concerned scholars understand the hardship of this kind of project, including procuring copies of manuscripts, reading of those texts, understanding those texts and editing. Apart from knowledge of Sanskrit, it requires special type of expertise. Fortunately, in the faculty of Sanskrit, R.B.U., there are scholars, teachers and fellows, who have achieved expertise in manuscriptologty and text-editing. The present edition is an outcome of the joint effort of the Department of Sanskrit R.B.U. While editing the texts (now on philosophy), we had no idea about the publication of these typical kind of texts, which are immensely important from academic point of view, but their market value is not viable. Around this time, a year ago, the co-ordinator met Professor Dr. Dipti Tripathi, Director of National Mission for Manuscripts (NMM), New Delhi, in a workshop on Manuscriptology in Tripura and discussed with her about the publication of these texts. Professor Tripathi, a dynamic academic personality, at once accepted our proposal and directed us about the procedure. The publication is going at last to see the light of the day and for which Professor Tripathi deserves highest credit. We are highly grateful to this Sanskrit scholar. Dr. Sanghamitra Basu, the publication co-ordinator of NMM, always extended her hand of co-operation during the publication procedure. We are also grateful to her. The chief editor Professor S.C. Goswami took the trouble and did his best to give the shape of the text. Research fellow Sm. Sujata Banerjee was always with Professor Goswami to help him in different phases of editing. She also deserves thanks. All teaching faculty of the department co-operated during the project, apart from their normal teaching-research work. I, personally, as a Co-ordinator of the project, thank them all. Myself, an outsider in the area of *Navya-Nyāya* philosophy, but by virtue of my office of co-rodinator, have to undertake the job. Concerned scholars should understand my hardship to write on this subject and forgive my lapses. I am fully aware of my limitations and shortcomings. Methodology of text-editing could not be achieved fully in spite of our best efforts. Yet, we are happy that finally the scholarship of an almost forgotten neo-logician Bengali Pandit Kaṇāda Tarkavagīśa finds the light of the day with the kind co-operation of National Mission for Manuscripts, New Delhi.

Consultant Editor
TARAK NATH ADHIKARI
Professor of Sanskrit and
Co-ordinator, DRS Project
(under SAP, UGC)
Rabindra Bharati University, Kolkata

Abbreviations

1. चिन्तामणि	Tattacintāmaṇi of Gaṇgeśa
2. काणादी	Kaṇādaṭippanī of Kaṇāda Tarkavāgīśa
3. Ms.	manuscript
4. का	Kaṇādaṭippanī/Kāṇādī.
5. चि	Cintāmaṇi i.e. Gaṇgeśa's work.
6. मूल (Mūla)	Tattvacintāmani of Gaṇgeśa
7. टिप्पणी (Ṭippanī)	Kaṇādaṭippaṇī
8. As I	G 785. (Catalogue-number of Asiatic Society) (G means Govt.-collection)
9. As 2	G 3504. (2nd manuscript of The Asiatic Society.)

Introduction

Nyāya-Vaiśeṣika Tradition

Among the many philosophical traditions developed in ancient India Nyāya forms an inportant group having a long journey since pre-christian era till the last decade of the twentieth century. Prācīna Nyāya, Vaiśeṣika and Navya-Nyāya—these three schools of Indian philosophy are included in this single tradition. Prācīna Nyāya took its full-fledged shape in the hands of Gautama or Akṣapāda, Vaiśeṣika started with the *Sūtra*-work of Kaṇāda and Navya-Nyāya emerged out of syncretism of both of them. Although it is a fact that Nyāya and Vaiśeṣka in the earlier stage had their separate identification, still they were regarded as co-sciences (*samānatantra*). This attitude resulted in the syncretism of both of them in later days and paved the way for the emergence of Navya-Nyāya as a distinguished school of philosophy. This last school of Nyāya-tradition contains the largest number of texts most of which are still lying unpublished.

Texts of Nyāya-literature are of two types, (1) independent works, and (2) commentaries. Independent works include texts written in *Sūtra*-form, in prose or verse form or in the mixed form. Commentaries may be written on an independent work, on a commentary or sub-commentary or sub-sub-commentary and so on. Large extent of this branch of learning developed mainly through series of commentaries.

Commentaries are not merely explanations of the lines of the given text. Commentators raise philosophical problems regarding a particular thesis and mention objections raised by opponent philosophers and even by philosophers of the same discipline and try to give solutions to them in their own way without hampering the philosophical structure of the school. Each commentator in this way shows personal ingenuity in handling a particular problem. Sometimes they venture to make amendments also of the theory mentioned in the basic text by way of new interpretation in order to save the thesis from being shattered by the counter-arguments of the opponents.

The first systematised work on Nyāya is the Nyāya-*Sūtra* of Gautama. This is an independent work. It was commented upon by Pakṣila Swāmī, also known as Vātsyāyana. This commentary of Vātsyāyana known as *Bhāṣya* was commented upon by Uddyotakara. His commentary known as *Vārttika* was commented upon by Vācaspati Miśra. His commentary is known as *Tātparyaṭīkā.* That too was commented upon by Udayanācārya. His commentary is known as *Pariśuddhi.* All these works from *Sūtra* to *Pariśuddhi* are now published. Other lines of commentaries might have existed at a time, but most of them are not traceable now. Śaṅkara, Sānātani, Trilocana, Aniruddha, Viṭṭoka and Śatānanda are few such names. *Vivaraṇapañjikā* of Aniruddha, a commentary on *Bhaṣya, Vārttika* and *Tātparyaṭīkā* has been discovered in the recent past. A school of Nyāya that advocated ten premises of Nyāya (syllogism) in lieu of five of the current school is known to have existed at a time. But no name or work belonging to that school is now known to us. Vardhamāna Upādhyaya, son of Gaṅgeśa Upādhyāya composed one large commentary known as *Prakāśa* on *Pariśuddhi.* From the works of Jayantabhaṭṭa and his commentator Cakradhara it is known that there were two main schools of Nyāya, one represented by Pravara and the other headed by Adhyayana.

The *Sūtra*-text is divided into five chapters. The first chapter deals with sixteen categories. Next three chapters are devoted to refuting the adverse criticism made by the opponents by way of examining the categories. The fifth chapter is introduced to elaborate the last two categories of *Jāti* (sophistical refutation) and *Nigrahasthāna* (defeat-situation). Gautama's *Sūtra*-work mainly served as a manual of the science of debate. Knowledge of sixteen categories mentioned in this text is a necessary precondition for successful performance in the parlance of philosophical disputations.

Among the independent works of Prācīna Nyāya mention may be made of Vāscapati Miśra's *Nyāyasūcīnibandha,* Udayanācārya's *Ātmatattvaviveka, Nyāyakusumāñjali, Prabodhasiddhi, Lakṣaṇamālā* and *Lakṣaṇāvali,* Jayantabhaṭṭa's *Nyāyamañjarī* and *Nyāyakalikā,* Varadarāja's *Tārkikarakṣā* etc.

One Bhāsarvajña of Kashmir in the ninth century AD composed *Nyāyasāra,* a work on Nyāya along with a commentary known as *Bhūsaṇa* on the same work. That was a very popular text and not less than eighteen commentaries were composed upon it. Jain writers also made attempts to write explanations of the text. But the content of the text partially deviates from the original work of Gautama and that is why the opinion of Bhāsarvajña was not totally accepted in the tradition in later days.

The *Sūtra*-text of Nyāya and even that of Vaiśeṣika suffered from misrepresentation in ancient times and they had to be corrected or put to order from time to time by susequent authors. In *Nyāya-sūcīnibandha* the sole aim of Vācaspati Miśra was to safeguard the tradition of *Nyāyasūtra* from going astray. *Kaṇādasūtra* the first Vaiśeṣika work also went into oblivion for a long time and Śaṅkara Miśra of Mithila (fifteenth century AD) for the first time reconstructed the text from materials available to him. Old commentaries of this book, i.e. *Rāvaṇabhāṣya* or *Kaṭandī, Bharadvājavṛtti* or Vṛtti are now lost. Śaṅkara Miśra wrote a commentary on *Kaṇādasūtra* known as *Upaskāra* which was subsequently commented upon by others. For example, Pañcānana Tarkaratna wrote a commentary known as *Pariṣkāra.* A Vṛtti text on *Vaiśeṣika Sūtra* written by Candrānanda has been discovered and published by Jamburijayaji in the Gaekwad Oriental Series No. 136. That is certainly much older than the *Upaskāra* of Śaṅkara Miśra. The *Sūtra* version in both these commentaries are not the same everywhere. Another old commentary of anonymous authorship has been edited and published by MM. Anantalal Thakur. But the *Sūtra*-tradition set by Śaṅkara Miśra went a long way before these discoveries were made. As a matter of fact Vaiśeṣika tradition in ancient days flourished in more than one school. From the Jaina literature it is known that *Kaṇāda Sūtra* had a brief commentary known as *Vākya* on which a *Bhāṣya* and a commentary by one Praśasta was existent at a time. Jaina author Mallavādi writes—'वाक्यं सभाष्यं प्रशस्तोऽन्यथा व्याचष्टे'. In Chinese Buddhist literature references of different schools of Vaiśeṣika are available, although no definite work has been restored yet.

In the absence of *Kaṇāda Sūtra* Praśastapāda's *Padārthadharma-saṁgraha* served the role of basic text of the Vaiśeṣika for a long time. The work is also known as *Praśastapādabhāṣya.* Though *Bhāṣya* by name it is actually a manual. *Kiraṇāvalī* of Udayanācārya, *Nyāyakandalī* of Śridharabhaṭṭa and *Vyomavatī* of Vyomaśivācārya are the three important old commentaries of the text. During the age of Navya-Nyāya in later period several commentaries were composed upon this book, such as *Setuṭīkā* of Padmanābha Miśra, *Sūkti* of Jagadīśā Tarkālṅkāra etc. *Nyāyalīlāvatī* of Vallabhācārya is another important text having a long chain of commentaries.

Saptapadārthī of Śivāditya Miśra, *Daśapadārthī* of Candra—these are also independent works of this philosophical tradition. Vyomaśivācārya in the Vaiśeṣika tradition was a writer of innovative character. He deviated from the traditional line on several occasions.

Both these traditions of ancient Nyāya and Vaiśeṣika fused together in course of time and formed another school of philosophy known as Navya-Nyāya. *Tattvacintāmaṇi* of Gangeśa Upādhyāya who hailed from Mithila in the beginning of the thirteenth century marks the advent of this new tradition. Śrīharṣa, the monistic Vedantist completely shattered the main tenets of Nyāya standardized at the hand of Udayanācārya by writing a book named *Khaṇḍanakhaṇḍakhādya.* This created a necessity for revitalisation of Nyāya tradition. At this juncture of time authors like Abhaya Tilaka, Maṇikaṇṭha, Śaśadhara, Keśava Miśra etc. tried to make stability of the system by writing books on Nyāya. Śaśadhara composed *Nyāyasiddhāntadīpa,* Keśava Miśra composed *Tarkabhāṣā* etc. But it was Gaṅgeśa who creditably succeeded to find out a new track for the establishment of Nyāya-tradition on a sound footing. Amalgamation of Nyāya and Vaiśeṣika was already in the process during Udayanācārya's time. The merger is completed in Gaṅgeśa's *Tattvacintāmaṇi.* From that time onwards the *Sūtra*-tradition set by Akṣapāda Gautama took the designation Prācīna Nyāya, that by Kaṇāda remained known as Vaiśeṣika and the newly originated tradition developed as a whole by Gaṅgeśopādhyāya became known as Navya-Nyāya. Thenceforth these three traditions continued to run side by side and are continuing till date.

Tattvacintāmaṇi the proclaimed basic text of Navya-Nyāya is divided into four parts-*Pratyakṣa* (perception), *Anumāna* (inference), *Upamāna* (Analogy), and *Śabda* (verbal testimony). It is based on the Ist category of Gautama's Nyāyasūtra (i.e. *Pramāṇa*). Bhāsarvajña's *Nyāyasāra* or *Pramānamīmāmsā* of Hemachandra Suri, an authoritative writer on Jaina philosophy might have been a model of this book. No work on any branch of Indian philosophy enjoyed so much popularity as that of *Cintāmaṇi* in Navya-Nyāya. Each and every topic of this book became the object of writing commentaries by the subsequent writers in later days. Study of Navya-Nyaya and writing explanatory works on a part or whole of the book became a symbol of respectful status and glory of the concerned scholar.

The *Pratyakṣa* section of *Tattvacintāmaṇi* contains the following topics: *Mangalavāda* (Theory of benediction), *Prāmāṇyavāda* (Validity of knowledge), *Anyathākhyātivāda* (Invalid knowldege), *Pratyakṣa-lakṣaṇa* (Definition of perception) *Sannikarṣavāda* (Theory of sense-object relation), *Laukika Pratyakṣa* (Ordinary perception), *Samavāyavāda* (Theory of inherent relation), *Abhāvavāda* (Non-existence), *Pratyakṣakāraṇavāda* (Causes of perception), *Mano'ṇutvavāda* (Atomic structure of the mind), *Anuvyavasāyavāda* (Doctrine of self-consciousness), *Nīrvikalpakavāda* (Indeterminate perception), *Savikalpakavāda* (Determinate perception) etc. In all, there are twelve sub-sections in this section. Upto *Anyathākhyātivāda* forms the general introduction to the whole text.

The *Anumāna* comprising seventeen sub-sections is the largest and most intricate section of the text. This section includes topics like *Anumiti* (Inferential cognition), Vyāptilakṣaṇa (Definitions of pervasion), *Vyāptigrahopāya* (Means of apprehending pervasion), *Vyāptyanugama* (Comprehensiveness of pervasion), *Sāmānyalakṣaṇā* (sense-object relation characterised by universal), *Upādhi* (Vitiating condition), *Pakṣatā* (Subjecthood in inference), *Parāmarśa* (Synthetic ascertainment of the reason), *Kevalānvayī* and *Kevalavyatirekī* (Inferences arising out of exclusively positive and exclusively negative pervasion), *Arthāpatti* (Postulation), *Svārthānumāna* and *Parārthānumāna* (Inference for one's self and for the sake of others). *Nyāyāvayava* (Syllogism and its constituents), *Sāmānyanirukti* (General definition of feigned reason i.e. fallacy), *Hetvābhāsa* (five kinds of fallacy with three subclasses), *Asādhakatāsādhakatva* (Efficiency of the fallacies in producing inefficiency of inference) and *Īśvarānumāna* (Inference of God). Practically speaking the *Anumāna* section is broadly divided into two halves commonly known as *Vyāptikāṇḍa* and *Jñānakāṇḍa.* The *Vyāptikāṇḍa* covers the portion from the beginning upto the end of *Sāmānyalakṣaṇā,* and the rest of the section commencing from Upādhi forms the second half namely *Jñānakāṇḍa.* Under the head *vyāpti* in the first half there are seven sub-sections namely *Vyāptipañcaka* (five provisional definitions of pervasion), *Siṁhavyāghrī* (two definitions of *Vyāpti* formulated by Professors known as Lion and Tiger), *Vyadhikaraṇadharmāvacchinnābhāva* (negation of something delimited by an attribute of different locus), *Pūrvapakṣa* (collection of other objectionable definitions of pervasion), *Siddhāntalakṣaṇa* (final definition of pervasion), *Sāmānyābhāva* (non-existence of the general form), and *Viśeṣavyapti* (Pervasion of special forms).

Upamāna-section is very short and contains no subsection. The Śabda-section is divided into sixteen subsections. The important topics discussed in this section are *Śabdanirūpaṇa* (Definition of verbal testimony), *Śābdabodha* (Verbal knowledge), *Śabdaprāmānyavāda* (Speech as a means of verbal knowledge), *Ākāṅkṣāvāda*

(Expectancy), *Yogyatāvāda* (Consistency), *Āsattivāda* (Continuity), *Tātparyavāda* (Intention), *Śabdānityatāvāda* (Non-eternity of sound), *Ucchannapracchannavāda* (the theory that sound when destroyed does not remain concealed), *Vidhivāda* (Injunction), *Apūrvavāda* (Theory of merit and demerit), *Śaktivāda* (Potentiality), *Lakṣaṇā* (Implication), *Samāsavāda* (Compound words), *Ākhyātavāda* (Verbal suffixes), *Dhātuvāda* (The roots), *Upasarga-vāda* (Prefixes), *Pramāṇacatuṣṭayaprāmāṇyavāda* [Validity of the four types of cognitive instruments alongwith refutation of so-called other Pramāṇas like tradition (*Aitihya*), rumour (*Janaśruti*), postulation (*Arthāpatti*) and non-apprehension (*Anupalabdhi*)].

Among the neo-logicians who contributed enormously to the development of this tradition in Mithila, Vardhamāna Upādhyāya, son of Gaṇgeśa, Śaṅkara Miśra, Vācaspati Miśra II, Yajñapati Upādhyāya, Jayadeva Miśra (also known as Pakṣadhara), Bhagīratha Ṭhakkura, Maheśa Ṭhakkura, Madhusūdan Ṭhakura, Gokulanāthopādhyāya etc. were prominent. Vardhamāna wrote extensive commentaries on the works of Udayana, Vallabhācārya, and Keśava Miśra, the author of *Tarkabhāṣā* and a critical exposition of Śriharṣa's work. An independent work *Anvīkṣānayatattvabodha* on the content of the fifth chapter of *Nyāya-Sūtra* also goes to his credit. No gloss on the text of Gaṅgeśa composed by him is known to have existed. A huge literature on *Tattvacintāmaṇi* alone developed due to the commentaries composed directly or indirectly by the Mithila authors. Among the independent works of this school during this period *Bhedaprakāśa* and *Vādivinoda* of Śaṅkara Miśra, *Nyāyasṣtroddhāra* and *Khaṇḍanoddhāra* of Vācaspati Miśra II are worth mentionable. Maximum number of commentaries were written on the *Tattvacintāmaṇi* of Gaṅgeśa, *Kiraṇāvalī* and *Kusumāñjali* of Udayanācārya and *Nyāyalilāvatī* of Vallabhācārya. *Āloka*-commentary of Jayadeva had the largest series of commentaries. The conflict between Yajnapati and his pupil Jayadeva contributed much to the development of this branch of learning. Later on, many scholars from Bengal School also wrote learned commentaries on the *Āloka* of Pakṣadhara The author of *Viveka*-commentary on the *Tattvacintāmaṇi* was another Pakṣadhara, according to Dr. D.C. Bhattacharya.

The Navya-Nyāya stream of philosophy that spread to Bengal in the meantime became enormously rich at the hands of a considerable number of outstanding Naiyāyiks. Vāsudeva Sārvabhauma is known to have started a seminary at Navadvipa and his pupil Raghunātha *Śrimoṇi* became famous for his brilliant commentary known as *Dīdhiti* on the text of Gaṅgeśa. In this work he made improvements or modifications of Gaṅgeśa's thesis on several occasions. In the tradition of Navya-Nyāya Raghunatha's innovative opinions are termed as *navyamata* (opinion of the new school of thought). Besides *Dīdhiti* on *Tattvacintāmaṇi* and on the works of Udayanācārya and Vallabhācārya he wrote three independent works like *Nañvāda*, *Ākhyātavāda* and *Padārtha-khaṇḍana* (also known as *Padārthatattvanirūpaṇa*). Scholars of next generation gave equal importance to *Cintāmaṇi* and *Dīdhiti* and wrote commentaries either on *Cintāmaṇi* or on *Didhiti* or on both. The seat of learning at Navadvipa was adorned mostly by Haridāsa Nyāyālaṅkāra, Jānakīnātha Tarkacūḍāmaṇi, Bhavānanda, Kṛḍṣṇadāsa Sārvabhauma, Mathurāṇātha, Jagadīśa, Harirāma, Gunānanda, Rāmabhadra, Viśvanātha Nyāyapañcānana and many other scholars patronised by the king of Navadvipa. The last doyen of such gigantic scholars was no other than Gadādhara Bhattāchārya in whom *Navya-Nyāya* rose to its highest peak. Among the independent treatises that have survived *Nyāyasiddhāntamañjarī* of Jānakinātha, *Śabdaśaktiprakāśikā* and *Tarkāmṛta* of Jagadīśa, *Kārakacakra* (probably a part of *Śabdārthavyākhyāsagǐaha*) of Bhavānanda, *Bhāṣāratna* of Kaṇāda Tarkavāgiśa, *Viṣayatāvāda* of Harirāma or Gadādhara, *Vyutpattivāda*, *Śaktivāda* and *Muktivāda* of Gadadhāra were very much popular in the seminaries.

This tradition continued vigorously till the advent of twentieth century. In the last stage of development a new type of writing came into existence knwon as *Vāda* or *Patrikā*. Authors of such works however, failed to produce any creative philosophical idea. Their dialectics dwelt upon a particular topic or passage of a particular work. Harirāma and Gadādhara had a considerable number of such *Vāda*-texts to their credit. Later on, Golokanātha gained fame of wide-range for his dialectics written mostly on the textual passages of Gadādhara's work. *Śankara Tarkavāgiśa* also was a Naiyāyika of repute in the post- Gadādhara period. Candranārāyana gained reputation as a *Patrikā*-writer at this time.

Kasi or Varanasi was a favourite place for settlement by Sanskrit schloars. Many Naiyāyikas coming from differrent parts of India started seminaries at Benaras during their staying here. Pragalbhācārya, Balabhadra Miśra, Padmanābha Miśra, Rudra Nyāyavācaspati, Jayarāma Nyāyapañcānana, Raghudeva Nyāyālaṅkāra, Annaṁbhaṭṭa and many other Naiyāyikas spent most of the creative period of their lives at this holy place, as a result of which some of the outstanding creations of *Navya-Nyāya* came into being at Benaras.

Tarkasaṁgraha, the popular primer of *Navya-Nyāya* written by Annaṁbhaṭṭa, a southern scholar was a product of this place. Another important primer text known as *Bhāṣāpariccheda* was very much popular and widely circulated and that came from the pen of Kṛṣṇadāsa Sārvabhauma or Viśvanātha Nyāyapañcānana perhaps at the holy place of Vṛndāvana.

Among the south-Indian scholars of *Navya-Nyāya* names of Chennu Bhaṭṭa, Mahādeva Punatāmakara, Nārāyna Tirtha, Kṛṣṇa Bhaṭṭa Āde, Mādhava Deva, Rājacūḍamaṇimakhin (Madras), Dharmarājādhvarin, Gopīnātha Mauni (Maharashtra), etc. come to the forefront. They and their followers contributed much to the development of *Navya-Nyāya* in this part of India. Some of them definitely left the mark of marvellous ingenuity in their number of works. *Tarkatāṇḍava* of Vyāsarāy, a dialectic on Mādhva logic played an important role for furtherance of *Navya-Nyāya* in the South.

From the observation of the vast literature of *Prācina Nyāya* and *Vaiśeṣika* it appears that the scholars belonging to these traditions had to fight vigorously against the adherents of opposing schools of philosophy primarily for establishing the concept of whole as different from that of the part, concept of universal and inherent relation, reality of non-existence, validity of inference, authority of the Veda, transitoriness of sound, eternal all-pervading soul as different from mind, body and sense-organs, earthly character of organic body, elemental character of sense-ograns, transient character of cognition, cognition as a quality of the soul, theory of origination of the prior non-existent, atomic character of the mind, qualified character of denotative meaning of a word, theory of Karma, merit and demerit, atomic origination of the Universe, God and His causality to Creation, and for refuting the theory of momentariness of objects, theory of absolute void, theory of consciousness arising out of conglomeration of elements, number of Pramāṇas in excess of four etc. However, on the last point there is disagreement between the two schools of Nyāya and *Vaiśeṣika. Vaiśeṣikas* admit only two *Pramāṇas*—perception and inference.

In *Navya-Nyāya* the main contenders for philosophical debate with Gaṅgeśa were the promulgators of Mīmāṁsā system of thought and logic. The major problems dealt with in *Tattvacintāmaṇi* were epistemic and Mimāṁsakas in this area belong to the other side of the stand taken by the Naiyāyikas. In the introductory portion of his text Gangesa discusses at length the problem of origination and ascertainment of validity of knowldege and the appropriate definitions of valid and invalid cognition (error) and in this context he cites textual references of the Mīmāśakas particularly of the Prabhākara school several times and refutes their views with minute details. In another place of his work he quotes the text of Jñānaśrimitra, a Buddhist scholar on the point of deliberating the reality of non-existence. But in most cases the identification of his opponent dialecticians remain unresolved. The peculiar method of Gaṅgeśa's writing provides a series of definitions of each topic which are to be made disqualified by his explanations and his own thesis is put in the long last in the form of final definition. The main business of Gaṅgeśa and his followers that stand in its present literature is to arrive at a correct definition of the concerned topic with all subtlety and perfection. The Naiyāyikas of this tradition themselves fight each other for propagating ingenuity and correctness of their definitions and ultimately becoming triumphant in the fault-finding game. For want of adequate evidences it becomes mostly impossible to trace the name of such rival logicians or their works and this happened in the case of Gaṅgeśa's text also. In the area of verbal testimony (i.e. language-philosophy) neo-grammarians of the Paninian school joined hands with the Mīmāṁsakas to throw some challenge to the Naiyayikas of later age.

Authors of Navya-Nyāya introduced several new concepts and technical terms bearing them for achieving perfection of their intending meaning. Few of such terms may be mentioned here. For example, *Avacchedakatva* (property of being the de-limotor of an attribute or of a relation), *Pratiyagitā* (property of being the countercorrelate of negation or of relation), *Anuyogitā* (relational or absential adjunctness), *Avyāpti* (under-extension), *Ativyāpti* (over-extension), *Upanitabhāna* (cognition produced by transcendent relation), *Pakṣadharmatā* (property of being present in the subject of inference), *Parāmarśa* (synthetic consideration of the reason), *Paryāpti* (sufficiency), *Viṣayatā* (objectivity), *Viṣayitā* (subjectivity), *Vyāsajyavṛtti* (inherent in conglomeration), *Vyāpyatva* (property of being narrow), *Vyāpakatva* (property of being wide), *Nirūpitatva* (property of the described), *Nirūpakatva* (property of the describer) *Prakāratā* (property of the characteriser), *Viśeṣyatā* (property of the characterised), *Saṁsargatā* (property of the relation), *Janyatā* (property of the produced), *Janakatā* (property of the producer), *Kāraṇatā* (causality), *Kāryatā* (property of the product) etc.

Masterly employment of combination of these concepts gives rise to the exactness of meaning intended by the Naiyāyikas resulting in prolongation and complexity of word-formation for which *Navya-Nyāya* has turned into a matter of horror to the general readers.

The complete picture of all the three traditions of *Nyāya* still remains somewhat cloudy. Innumerable writings have already gone into oblivion. Some of them and their authors are known at present only by name. Sanskrit writers in most cases left no record of their personal lives or of their writings for the posterior. Researches are going on in and outside India and a good number of books and papers have already been published from different places. On the basis of materials collected so far the researchers are stretching their power of conjecture and imagination to build up the history of this rich cultural traditon.

The main task now lying before us is to collect manuscripts of this branch of learning that still remain to be found out from all possible hide-outs and at the same time to edit and publish collected manuscripts waiting for long to see the light of the day. Evaluation of contributions made by individual authors can be carried out successfully in the next stage and then only faithful reconstruction of this ancient culture will be made possible. Failure of preparing catalogues of innumerable manuscripts collected and deposited even in the well-organised libraries of India and European countries is a matter of grave concern. Had that been properly done by this time many new things would surely come out which might have contributed much to the progress of our research-activity.

Kaṇāda Tarkavāgiśa and His Works

It has already been stated earlier that Kaṇāda Tarkavāgiśa is one among those prominent representatives of Bengal School of Navya-Nyāya. According to Dr. D. C. Bhattacharya this Kaṇāda was a fellow-student of Raghunāth Śiromaṇi and he flourished in the Khanakul-Kraishnanagar of Bengal during the second half of fifteenth century to the first part of sixteenth century AD. The same view is maintained by MM. Haraprasad Śastri also (vide-*Mānasī O Marmavāṇi*, Kartick issue, B.S. 1331, page 220). The first editor of West Bengal District Gazetter, Hooghly also subscribes to the same opinion regarding his time and mentions one Bansidhar Roy to be his patron.

It appears from the information of Catalogus Catalogorum of Aufrecht and New Catalogus Catalogorum that Kaṇāda wrote at least four works on Navya-Nyāya-(1) *Bhāṣāratnam,* (2) *Tarkavādārthamañjari,* (3) *Apaśabdakhaṇḍanam,* and (4) *Anumānacintāmaṇitippanī.* On scrutiny it has been detected that *Apaśabdakhaṇḍanam* is not the outcome of Kaṇāda's pen. It was written by one Kanotka. The work has been edited with rendering into English and published by the present author in the Journal of the Department of Sanskrit, Rabindra Bharati Bharati University (Vol. VI). Manuscript copy of *Tarkavādārthamañjarī* is yet to be recovered. Manuscripts in the collection of Sanskrit Sahitya Parishat, Calcutta under the title of *Tarkavādārthamañjari* have been verified by the present scholar and proved to be a case of wrong entry. The text of *Bhāṣāratnam* has been edited and commented upon by M.M. Kālipada Tarkācārya. The book is published by the Sanskrit Sahitya Parishat, Kolkata *Anumānacintāmaṇitippanī* is not available in its complete form. Two copies of the manuscript belong to the collections of the Asiatic Society of Bengal. Both the copies contain only fragments of the work with internal omissions also. *Pakṣatā*-section of *Tippanī* is wanting in both of those two bundles of manuscripts. Accidentally the present scholar detected the existence of one copy of *Pakṣatāṭippanī* in the collections of Govt. Sanskrit College, Kolkata and forthwith edited the copy with rendering into English. That was published in the third volume of the Journal of the Department of Sanskrit, Rabindra Bharati University, Kolkata (1986-88). The present volume contains an improved version of that edition. Editing of *Sāmānyanirukti* is a new attempt. Both *Pakṣatācintāmaṇiṭippanī* and *Sāmānyaniruktiṭippanī* are parts of the larger text *Anumānacintāmaṇiṭippanī* of Kaṇāda. Construction of other parts of the text will be possible only on availability of adequate and trustworthy materials.

Part I

Pakṣatācintāmaṇi of Gaṅgeśa

with

Kaṇādaṭippaṇī

Mūla, Ṭippaṇī & English translation

Editorial Note

The present text better known as *Kāṇādī* is based upon a single manuscript available so far and that is kept in the library of Government Sanskrit College, Calcutta (vide A Descriptive Catalogue of Sanskrit Manuscripts, Vol. I Part III, Page 808, No. 946/414). The manuscript is described there as such: "Pakṣatāṭīkā by Kaṇāda Tarkavāgīśa. Substance—country-made yellow paper. Size—18¼ x 3¼ inches. Folios-4(1a-4a). Neatly written in Bengali character. 8-11 lines in a page. Extent about 240 ślokas. Appearance—old. Prose. Incorrect. Complete." Condition of the manuscript is not tolerable now. With the destruction of this manuscript the text might have been out of sight for ever. The manuscript copy is incorrect occasionally and mode of writing is not clearly legible somewhere. Lack of appropriate punctuation and continuity of writing leaving no gap between words sometimes stand problematic in the task of construction of the text. But one point of advantage is that it is a commentary work in nature and the original work *Pakṣatācintāmaṇī* is available in a number of printed editions. Corrections have been made possible in a number of occasions only with the help of this source book. In fact, writers on Navya-Nyāya deal with their topics mostly with a set of words peculiar to their own literature and they are inclined to stress upon the clarity of expression and not upon the ornamentation of language. The peculiar argumentative language and the frequent use of a set of peculiar words and technical terms of their own render much help to a scholar of Navya-Nyāya in constructing any Navya-Nyāya text from manuscript sources with much confidence and certainty.

The manuscript copy is certainly not the autograph of the author but only a transcript copy of the same and it is not certain whether it is directly descended from the autograph copy or from a transcribed copy of any intermediate stage.

In translation work, English synonyms of Sanskrit technical terms have been collected mostly from standard books on Navya-Nyāya. Innovation of any sort has been indicated by putting the corresponding Sanskrit word side by side in a bracket.

पक्षताचिन्तामणि काणादी च

पक्षताचिन्तामणि–१

व्याप्त्यनन्तरं पक्षधर्मता निरूप्यते। तत्र न तावत् सन्दिग्धसाध्यधर्मत्वं* पक्षत्वम्। सन्देहो हि न विशेषणं, परामर्शपूर्वं लिंगदर्शनव्याप्तिस्मरणादिना तस्य नाशात्। नोपलक्षणम् अव्यावर्तकतापत्तेः। नापि साधकबाधकमाना[1] भावः उभयाभावस्य प्रत्येकसत्त्वेऽपि सत्त्वात्। नाप्यभावद्वयं तथा, बाधकप्रमाणा[2] भावस्य व्यर्थत्वात्। ह्रदादेः पक्षत्वेऽपि बाधहेत्वसिद्ध्यादेरावश्यकत्वेनानुमित्य-नुत्पादात्।**

काणादी 1

(a) ॐ नमो गणेशाय। व्याप्तीति व्याप्त्यनन्तरं व्याप्तिनिरूपणानन्तरं पक्षधर्मता पक्षे धर्मता यस्याः पक्षरूपो यो धर्मस्तस्य भावः इति व्यत्पत्त्या वा पक्षता निरूप्यत इत्यर्थः। अतः पक्षतानिरूपणेनार्थान्तरम्। अनुमितिरूपएककार्यकारित्वसंगत्या पक्षतां निरूपयितुं शिष्यावधानाय प्रतिजानीते। ज्ञापनं ज्ञानानुकूलव्यापारः शब्दप्रयोगरूपः। अत्र व्याप्तिपदे व्यप्तिनिरूपणे लक्षणा। अनन्तरपदस्य च ध्वंसादिकारणकानुवृत्तिरर्थः। तदेकदेशे च ध्वंसे व्याप्तिपदार्थस्य व्याप्तिनिरूपणस्य प्रतियोगिता अन्वयः। आख्यातार्थो विषयत्वम्। विषयता च व्यापारानुबन्धिनाम्। अतः शब्दस्य निर्विषयत्वेऽपि न क्षतिः। तथा च व्याप्तिनिरूपणध्वंसादिकरणकानुवृत्तिनिरूपणविषयः पक्षता इत्यन्वयबोधः। तत्र निरूपणे सप्तम्यर्थो विषयत्वम्, तस्य च पक्षत्वमित्यनेनान्वयः।

(b) सन्दिग्धेति। सन्दिग्धः साध्यरूपो धर्म्मो यस्य इति व्युत्पत्त्या सन्दिग्ध-साध्यवत्त्वधर्मवत्त्वं साध्यतावच्छेदकसम्बन्धावच्छिन्नाधेयत्वं साध्ये सन्दिग्धमिति यावत्, स तादात्म्येन पक्षत्वमिति वार्थः। भवति च वह्न्यादौ संयोगसम्बन्धावच्छिन्नाधेयत्वं पर्व्वतादिनिरूपितं सन्दिग्धमिति तादात्म्येन पर्व्वतादेरेव[3] पक्षतेति। न च व्याप्यनिश्चय-मप्युक्तम्। आद्ये अतीतानागतवह्न्यादिविधेयकानुमितौ पक्षताविरहप्रसंगात्। अनुमित्यव्यवहितप्राक्काले पर्वतादौ सन्दिग्धवह्न्यादिमत्त्वाभावात्। द्वितीये अतीतानागतपक्षकानुमितौ पक्षताविरहप्रसंगात्। यत्र तमसि समवायेन आकाशं साध्यं तत्र पक्षताविरहप्रसंगाच्च। तमोनिरूपितसमवायसम्बन्धावच्छिन्नाधेयत्वस्याप्रसिद्धेः। यत्तु

साध्यसन्देहत्वपक्षता इत्याह तदपि न, साध्यविशेष्यकसाध्यप्रकारकोभयसाधारण-साध्यसंशयत्वस्य अनुगतस्यैकस्य वक्तुमशक्यत्वात्। पक्षविशेष्यकसाध्यप्रकारक-निश्चयप्रतिबन्ध्यं यत् पक्षसाध्योभयावगाहिज्ञानं तत् पक्षतेत्यत्र तात्पर्यात्। भवति च पर्वतो वह्निमान् इति निश्चयप्रतिबध्यो पर्व्वतो वह्निमान्नवेति संशयो वह्निः पर्व्वते न वेति संशयश्चोभौ च। वह्निपर्व्वतोभयवैशिष्ट्यावगाहिना विहितयोर्द्वयोरेव पक्षतात्वम्। पर्व्वतवह्न्युभयवैशिष्ट्यावगाहितया तस्य पक्षतात्ववारणाय प्रतिबध्यान्तम्।

(c) पर्व्वतो वह्न्यभाववानिति बाधनिश्यस्यापि पर्व्वतविशेष्यकवह्निप्रकारकनिश्चय-प्रतिबध्यतया तस्य पक्षतात्वापत्तिः। अतो विशेष्यदलम्। न च बाधनिश्चयस्य पक्षतात्वेऽपि न क्षतिः, ततः सत्त्वे अनुमित्यापत्तिस्तु अनुमितिं प्रति बाधनिश्चयस्य प्रतिबन्धकत्वादेव[4] निरसनीयेति वाच्यम्। अनुमितिं प्रति हि अप्रामाण्यज्ञानानास्कन्दित-बाधनिश्चय एव विरोधीति यत्रादौ अप्रामाण्यज्ञानास्कन्दितबाधनिश्चयत्वं तत्र अनुमित्यापत्तेर्दुर्व्वारत्वात् बाधनिश्चयरूपपक्षतासत्त्वात् अप्रामाण्यज्ञानानास्कन्दितबाध-निश्चयाभावसत्त्वाच्च।

(d) अत्र च साध्यत्वादेरेकस्याभावात् विशिष्टैव पक्षता वाच्या। तथाहि पर्वतत्वावच्छिन्नविशेष्यतानिरूपितसंयोगनिष्ठसांसर्गिकविषयतानिरूपितवह्नित्वावच्छिन्नप्रकारताक-निश्चयप्रतिबध्यत्वे सति पर्वतत्वावच्छिन्नविषयतानिरूपितवह्नित्वावच्छिन्नविषयकज्ञानत्वं पर्वतत्वावच्छिन्नविशेष्यतानिरूपितसंयोगनिष्ठसांसर्गिकविषयतानिरूपितवह्नित्वावच्छिन्नविधेयकानुमितौ पक्षतात्वम्। समवायेन पर्वतवह्निसंशयात्[5] संयोगेन पर्वते वह्नित्वमिति वारणाय संयोग-निष्ठसांसर्गिकविषयताकत्वत्त्वेशः।

(e) यथाश्रुतं दूषयति सन्देहो हीति। लिंगदर्शनव्याप्तिस्मरणादिना लिंगदर्शन-व्याप्तिस्मरणाद्यन्यतमेन तस्य सन्देहस्य नाशादिति। यत्रादौ लिंगदर्शनं ततो व्याप्तिस्मरणं ततः परामर्शः तत्र लिंगदर्शनात् संशयनाशः। यत्र च आदौ व्याप्तिस्मरणं ततो लिंगदर्शनं तत्र व्याप्तिस्मरणात् संशयनाशः। तथाचानुमितेः पूर्व्वं संशयविशिष्टसाध्याभावात् न तस्य पक्षतात्वमिति भावः।

(f) ननु यदा कदाचित् संशयविषयसाध्यवत्त्वमेव पक्षतेति नोक्तदोष इत्याशङ्क्य निराकरोति नोपलक्षणमिति। व्यावर्त्तकतापत्तेः सपक्षाव्यावर्त्तकतापत्तेः।[6] तथाच पर्वतो वह्निमानिति निश्चयसत्त्वेऽपि पर्व्वतो वह्निमानित्यनुमित्युत्पादापतेः। यदा कदाचित् संशयविषयवह्निमत्त्वस्य तदानीमपि पर्व्वते सत्त्वादिति भावः, परामर्शपूर्व्वं संशयस्य नाशात् निष्कृष्टलक्षणमपि निरस्तम्। न च संशययोग्यत्वमेव पक्षता, संशयासत्त्वेऽपि तदयोग्यतायाः सत्त्वात् नोक्तदोष इति वाच्यम्। योग्यत्वानुगतयो[7] रेकस्य वक्तुमशक्यत्वात्।

(g) कस्यचिल्लक्षणं दूषयति–नापीति। साधकेत्यादि।[8] मान[9] मितिः प्रमितिः। अप्रामाण्यज्ञानानास्कन्दित इति यावत्। तथा चाप्रामाण्यज्ञानानास्कन्दितसिद्धिनिश्चय-बाधनिश्चययोरभावः पक्षतेत्यर्थः। न च केवलान्वयिनि साध्याभावाप्रसिद्ध्या बाधनिश्चयासम्भव इति वाच्यम्। घटवृत्त्यभावस्थले वाच्यत्वप्रतियोगित्वभ्रमेण घटो

न वाच्य इति बाधनिश्चयसम्भवात्।

(h) ननु सिद्धिबाधनिश्चयाभावस्य सिद्धिबाधनिश्ययोभयत्वावच्छिन्नप्रतियोगिताकाभाववत्त्वेन हेतुत्वम्, किंवा असिद्ध्यभावत्वेन बाधनिश्चयाभावत्वेन च हेतुत्वम्। तत्राद्यं दूषयति उभयाभावस्येति। सिद्धिबाधनिश्चयोभयत्वावच्छिन्नप्रतियोगिताकाभावस्येत्यर्थः। प्रत्येकसत्त्वेऽपि सिद्धिबाधनिश्चययोरेकमात्रसत्त्वेऽपि सत्त्वादिति। तथाच सिद्धिकालीनबाधनिश्चयाभावदशायां बाधनिश्चयकालीनसिद्ध्यभावदशायां वा अनुमित्युत्पादापत्तिरिति भावः। द्वितीयं दूषयति–नापीति। अभावद्वयमिति सिद्ध्यभावो बाधनिश्चयाभावश्चेत्यर्थः। बाधकप्रमाणाभावस्येति अप्रामाण्यज्ञानास्कन्दितबाधनिश्चयाभावस्येत्यर्थः।

(i) ननु सिद्ध्यभावमात्रस्य पक्षतात्वे ह्रदो वह्न्यभाववानिति बाधनिश्चयदशायां ह्रदो वह्निमानित्यनुमितिः कुतो न जायत इत्यत आह ह्रदादेरिति। बाधहेत्वसिद्ध्यादेरिति। बाधो बाधनिश्चयः, हेत्वसिद्धिः हेतोः पक्षावृत्तित्वज्ञानम्। आदिपदात् सत्प्रतिपक्षपरिग्रहः। आवश्यकत्वेन अवश्यक्लृप्तअनुमित्यनुत्पादप्रयोजकत्वेन अनुमित्यनुत्पादात् अनुमित्यापत्तिवारणसम्भवात्। तथा च सिद्ध्यभावमात्रस्य पक्षतात्वे न कोऽपि दोष इति भावः।

चिन्तामणि 2

नापि साधकप्रमाणा[10] भावः, श्रोतव्यो मन्तव्यो इति श्रुत्या समानविषयकश्रवणानन्तरं मननबोधनात् प्रत्यक्षदृष्टेऽप्यनुमानदर्शनात् एकलिंगावगतेऽपि लिंगान्तरेण तदनुमानाच्च, मन्तव्यश्चोपपत्तिभिरिति श्रवणात्*।**

काणादी 2

(a) ननु यद्येवं सिद्ध्यभावमात्रं पक्षता तथापि पक्षतानिरूपणं कथमिति दूषयति नापीत्यादि। साधकप्रमाणाभावः अप्रामाण्यज्ञानानास्कन्दितसिद्ध्यभाव इत्यर्थः। श्रोतव्यो मन्तव्य इति आत्मा वाऽरे श्रोतव्यो मन्तव्यो निदिध्यासितव्य आत्मा साक्षात् द्रष्टव्य इति श्रुत्या इत्यर्थः। समानविषयेकेति। आत्मविषयकशाब्दबोधानन्तरमित्यर्थः। मननबोधनादिति आत्मविषयकानुमितिबोधनादित्यर्थः। तथा च शाब्दबोधात्मकसिद्धिसत्त्वे सिद्ध्यभावासत्त्वात् अनुमितिर्न स्यादिति भावः।

(b) ननु प्रात्यक्षिकसिद्ध्यभावमात्रं पक्षता वाच्येति नोक्तदोष इत्यत आह प्रत्यक्षेति। प्रात्यक्षिकसिद्धिसत्त्वेऽपि सिषाधयिषातोऽनुमितिदर्शनादित्यर्थः। तथा च तत्र सिद्ध्यभावासत्त्वात् अनुमितिर्न स्यादिति भावः। केचित्तु–ननु श्रोतव्य इत्यादिश्रुत्या शाब्दबोधानन्तरमेव अनुमितिर्बोधिता न तु शाब्दबोधाव्यवहितोत्तरं, तच्च शाब्दबोधानन्तरमपि सम्भवति। अतो दूषणान्तरमाह प्रत्यक्षदृष्टेऽपीति। व्याख्यातमेतदित्याहुः।

(c) ननु अनुमित्यात्मकसिद्ध्यभावमात्रं पक्षता वाच्येति नोक्तदोष इत्यत आह एकलिंगके तदनुमितिसत्त्वेऽपि इत्यर्थः। तदनुमानात् तदनुमित्युत्पादात्। ननु एकलिंगकानुमितिसत्त्वे अन्यलिंगकानुमितिरसिद्धा इत्यत आह मन्तव्यश्चेति। मन्तव्यः अनुमातव्यः उपपत्तिभिः नानासाधनैः। यद्यपि एकलिंगकानुमितिनाशानन्तरम् अन्यलिंगकानुमित्युत्पादेऽपि मन्तव्य इत्यादिश्रुत्यर्थनिर्वाहः सम्भवति तथापि एकलिंगकानुमितिसत्त्वेऽपि यत्रान्यलिंगकानुमितिः तत्र अनुमित्यात्मकसिद्ध्यभावासत्त्वात् अनुमितिर्न स्यादित्येव दूषणं द्रष्टव्यम्। न च धूमलिंगकपर्वतत्वधर्मितावच्छेदकवह्नि-विधेयकानुमित्यभावः धूमलिंगकपर्वतत्वधर्मितावच्छेदकवह्निविधेयकानुमितौ पक्षतेति रीत्या पक्षता निर्वाच्या इति वाच्यम्। यत्रानुमितिद्वयं जायतामितीच्छया वह्निव्या-प्यधूमवत्पर्व्वतनिश्चयानन्तरम् अनुमितिद्वयं तत्र द्वितीयानुमित्यनुत्पादापत्तेः। तस्या अपि धूमलिंगकपर्वतत्वधर्मितावछेदकवह्निविधेयकानुमितित्वात्। तत्पूर्वञ्च धूमलिंगकपर्वतत्वधर्मितावछेदकवह्निविधेयकानुमित्यभावाभावात् इति।

चिन्तामणि 3

अत्र सिषाधयिषितसाध्यधर्माधर्म्मी पक्षः। तथाहि मुमुक्षोः शब्दादात्मावगमेऽपि मननस्य मोक्षोपायत्वेन सिद्धिविशेषानुमितीच्छया आत्मानुमानम्। अतएव 'प्रत्यक्षपरिकल्पितमप्यर्थमनुमानेन वुभुत्सन्ते तर्करसिकाः' 'न हि करिणि दृष्टे चीत्कारेण तमनुमिमतेऽनुमातारः' इति वाचस्पतिवचनयोरविरोधः।

काणादी 3

सिषाधयिषितेति। अनुमितीच्छाविषयीभूतसाध्यवत्त्वं पक्षत्वमित्यर्थः। न चातीनानागतविधेयकानुमितौ व्यभिचारः। तत्पूर्वम् अनुमितीच्छाविषयीभूतसाध्याभावा-दिति वाच्यम्। साध्यसिद्धीच्छाया अपेक्षितात्वे तात्पर्यात्। अतएव साध्यत्वादेरनुगत-स्यैकस्याभावात् पर्वतधर्मितावच्छेदकवह्निविधेयकानुमितौ पर्वतत्वधर्मितावच्छेदक-वह्निविधेयकानुमितीच्छा पक्षतेति पक्षता निर्वाच्येति। लक्ष्ये लक्षणं संगमयति तथाहीति। सिद्धिविशेषेति। अनुमित्यात्मको यः सिद्धिविशेषः तदिच्छया इत्यर्थः। अतएवेति। सिषाधयिषाया अनुमितिहेतुत्वादेवेत्यर्थः। तदुपपत्तेः तयोर्वाक्ययोरविरोधोपपत्तेः।

चिन्तामणि 4

अनुमित्सातद्विरहाभ्यां तदुपपत्तेरिति चेन्न। सन्देहवत् परामर्शपूर्वं सिषाधयिषाया अप्यभावात् योग्यतायाश्चानिरूपणात् सिषाधयिषाविरहेऽपि घनगर्जितेन मेघानुमानात् स्वकारणाधीनतृतीयलिंगपरामर्शबलेन अनपेक्षितानुमान-दर्शनाच्चेति।

काणादी 4

(a) सन्देहवदिति, सन्देहस्यैवेत्यर्थः। सिषाधयिषाया अपीति व्याप्तिस्मरणादिनेत्यर्थः। अभावात् नाशात्। तथाच व्यभिचारात् सिषाधयिषाया न हेतुत्वमिति भावः। न च तत्र अनुमित्सान्तरोत्पत्तिः ततोऽनुमितिरित्यत आह सिषाधयिषाविरहेऽपीति। मेघानुमितीच्छाविरहेऽपीत्यर्थः। तेन विजातीयशब्देन मेघानुमानादिति। अयं कालो मेघवान् विजातीयशब्दवत्त्वादित्यनुमानादित्यर्थः। ननु तत्रापि सिषाधयिषोत्पत्तौ बाघकाभावात् सिषाधयिषाविरहोऽसिद्ध[11] एव इत्यत आह स्वकारणाधीनेति। स्वं तृतीयलिंगपरामर्शः। तस्य कारणं यद्व्याप्तिस्मरणादि तदधीनेत्यर्थः।

(b) ननु परामर्शबलेन इत्येवोच्यतां, किं स्वकारणाधीनत्वाभिधानेनेति वाच्यम्। परामर्शस्य इच्छाधीनत्व[12] प्रतिपादनार्थं तदभिधानात्। परामर्शस्य इच्छाधीनत्वे तत्रानुमितीच्छाया आवश्यकतापत्तेः। उपायेच्छां प्रति फलेच्छाया हेतुत्वात्। अनपेक्षितेति। इच्छाधीनत्वेन निश्चितत्वे अनुमानदर्शनादित्यर्थः।

तथाच अनुमितिर्नेष्टसाधनमिति निश्चयसत्त्वे अनुमितीच्छोत्पादासम्भवात् अनुमितेश्च तत्रानुभवसिद्धत्वात् व्यभिचारत्वेन सिषाधयिषाया न हेतुत्वमिति भावः।

चिन्तामणि 5

उच्यते। सिषाधयिषाविरहसहकृतसाधक[13] प्रमाणाभावो यत्रास्ति स पक्षः। तेन सिषाधयिषाविरहसहकृतं साधकप्रमाणं यत्रास्ति स न पक्षः। यत्र साधकप्रमाणे सत्यसति वा सिषाधयिषा यत्र वोभयाभावस्तत्र विशिष्टाभावात् पक्षत्वम्।

काणादी 5

(a) सिषाधयिषाविरहेति। सिषाधयिषाविरहविशिष्टं यत् साधकप्रमाणं तस्याभावः पक्षतेत्यर्थः। सिषाधयिषा अनुमितीच्छा, साधकप्रमाणम्[14] अप्रामाण्यज्ञानाभावविशिष्टा-सिद्धिः न कार्यस्य, अविवक्षितत्वात्। प्रमाणपदस्य भावव्युत्पत्त्या प्रमितिपरतया अप्रामाण्यज्ञानानास्कन्दितत्वलाभात् सिद्धिः। पक्षतावच्छेदकरूपेण पक्षे साध्यतावच्छेदक-रूपेण साध्यनिश्चयः। पाषाणमयो वह्निमान् इति निश्चयसत्त्वे विनापि सिषाधयिषां पर्व्वतो वह्निमान् इत्यनुमित्युत्पादात् पक्षतावच्छेदकप्रवेशः। पर्व्वतस्तेजस्वीति निश्चयसत्त्वेऽपि विनापि सिषाधयिषां पर्व्वतो वह्निमान् इत्यनुमित्युत्पादात् साध्यतावच्छेदकप्रवेशः। एकसम्बन्धेन सिद्धिसत्त्वे विनाप्यनुमित्साम् अपरसम्बन्धेन अनुमित्युत्पादात् सम्बन्धनिवेशोऽपि कार्यः। यत्रादौ सिषाधयिषा ततः पर्व्वतो वह्निमान् वह्निव्याप्यवांश्च पर्व्वत इति सधूमालम्बनपरामर्शः ततोऽनुमितिस्तत्र सिद्ध्यभावाभावात् पक्षतासम्पत्तये विशिष्टान्तं सिद्धौ विशेषणम्। तथाच तत्र सिषाधयिषाभावरूपविशेषणाभाव-कृतविशिष्टाभावसत्त्वात् पक्षतासत्त्वमिति।

(b) न च यत्किंचित्गोचरं ज्ञानं जायतामिति इच्छातोऽपि सिद्धिसत्त्वे अनुमितिः स्यात्, तस्या अपि अनुमितिविषयकेच्छात्वात्। न चानुमितित्वप्रकारकेच्छैव उत्तेजिकेति

वाच्यम्। प्रत्यक्षाद्यतिरिक्तं ज्ञानं जायतामिति इच्छातोऽपि सिद्धात्मकपरामर्शात् अनुमित्युत्पादात् इति वाच्यम्। यादृशयादृशेच्छासत्त्वे सिद्धिसत्त्वे अनुमितिस्तदभावकूट-विशिष्टसिद्ध्यभावत्वेन हेतुतायाः विवक्षितत्वात्। न च यादृशाभावकूटानां परस्परं विशेषणविशेष्यभावे विनिगमनाविरहेण बहुतरकार्य्यकारणभावत्वेनापत्तिरिति वाच्यम्। अन्यथा[15] अपि तस्याः स्वीकारात्।

(c) अत्र च पक्षत्वादेरेकस्य अभावात् विशिष्टैव पक्षता निर्व्वाच्या। तथाच पर्व्वतत्वावच्छिन्नविशेष्यतानिरूपितसंयोगनिष्ठसांसर्गिकविषयतानिरूपितवह्नित्वावच्छिन्नविधेयकानुमितौ तावदिच्छाभावकूटविशिष्टस्य प्रामाण्यप्रसंगात् कूटविशिष्टस्य पर्व्वतत्वावच्छिन्नविशेष्यता-निरूपितवह्नित्वावच्छिन्नप्रकारताकनिश्चयस्य अभावः पक्षता। एवमन्यत्रापि पर्व्वतो वह्निमानिति निश्चयसत्त्वे विनापि सिषाधयिषां वह्निमत्पर्व्वतो द्रव्यम् इत्याद्यनुमित्युत्पादात् तत्र व्यभिचारवारणाय प्रकारतामपहाय विधेयतायाः प्रवेशः। तथाच तत्र वह्नेर्विधेयत्वाभावान्न व्यभिचारः। विधेयता च अनुमिनोमीत्यनुव्यवसायसाक्षिकः प्रकारताविशेषः।

(d) अत्र च पर्व्वतत्वसामानाधिकरण्येन पर्व्वतो वह्निमानिति सिद्धिसत्त्वेऽपि विनानुमित्साम् अवच्छेदकावच्छेदेन पर्व्वतो वह्निमानिति अनुमित्युत्पादात् अवच्छेदकावच्छेदेन अनुमितिं प्रति अवच्छेदकावच्छेदेन सिद्धेः प्रतिबन्धकत्वं वाच्यम्। पक्षतावच्छेदकावच्छिन्नञ्च पक्षतावच्छेदकव्यापकत्वं तत्र प्रकारे संसर्गाभावादेव भासते। स्वावच्छेदकसामानाधिकरण्येन अनुमितिं प्रति तु पक्षतावच्छेदकसामानाधिकरण्येन पक्षतावच्छेदकावच्छेदेन च सिद्धिः प्रतिबन्धिका। पक्षतावच्छेदकसामानाधिकरण्येन अनुमितिस्तु संयोगादिपर्याप्तसांसर्गिकविषयताकानुमितिर्वा। इत्थञ्च पर्व्वतत्वावच्छिन्न-विषयतानिरूपितपर्वतत्वाव्यापकत्वावच्छिन्नविधेयताकानुमितित्वेन प्रतिबध्यता। सिषा-धयिषाविरहविशिष्टअप्रामाण्य[16] ज्ञानाभावविशिष्टपर्वत्वावच्छिन्नविशेष्यतानिरूपित-पर्वतत्वाव्यापकत्वावच्छिन्नसंयोगनिष्ठसांसर्गिकविषयतानिरूपितवह्नित्वावच्छिन्नप्रकारताक-निश्चयत्वेन प्रतिबन्धकता। अत्र च अवच्छेदकावच्छेदेन अनुमितिश्चैव उत्तेजिका वा बोध्या। एवं पर्व्वतत्वावच्छिन्नविशेष्यतानिरूपितसंयोगपर्य्याप्त[17] सांसर्गिकविषयता-निरूपितवह्नित्वावच्छिन्नविधेयताकानुमितित्वेन पर्व्वतत्वावच्छिन्नविशेष्यतानिरूपित-पर्व्वतत्वव्यापकत्वानवच्छिन्नसंयोगनिष्ठसांसर्गिकविषयताकानुमितित्वेन वा प्रतिबन्ध्यता इति रीत्या प्रतिबध्यप्रतिबन्धकभावाः कल्पनीया इति।

(e) प्रतिबन्धकतावच्छेदककोटौ यादृश-यादृशइच्छासत्त्वे सिद्धौ सत्यामनुमितिस्त-दिच्छाभावसमदायो न निवेश्यः। किन्त स्वप्रागभावबोधकत्वसामानाधिकरण्योभयसम्बन्धेन पर्व्वतत्वधर्मितावच्छेदकवह्न्यविधेयकानुमितिविशिष्टा या कृतिः[18] सामानाधिकरण्य-सम्बन्धेन तद्विशिष्टा या इच्छा तत्सामान्याभाव एव निवेश्यः। यादृश-यादृश-इच्छासत्त्वे पर्व्वतो वह्निमानिति सिद्धिसत्त्वे[19] पर्व्वतो वह्निमानित्यनुमितिः तादृशानां सर्व्वासामेब इच्छानाम् उक्तजातिमत्त्वादिति नव्याः। वस्तुतस्तु सिद्धिविशिष्टान्यानुमितिं प्रति सिद्धत्वेन प्रतिबन्धकत्वं सिषाधयिषानुमितिं च सिषाधयिषाया हेतुत्वम्। उभयत्व[20] वैशिष्ट्यं स्वाधेयप्रागभावप्रतियोगित्वसामानाधिकरण्योभयसम्बन्धेन। तत्रैच स्वत्वं न सम्बन्धता-

वच्छेदकेन निवेश्य[21] किन्तु परिचायकमात्रम्, एकाधेयप्रागभावप्रतियोगित्वस्य अन्यसम्बन्धत्वाभावात्, विस्तरस्तु अस्माकं *तर्कवादार्थमञ्जर्यामनुसन्धेयः।

(f) ननु समवायेन अनुमितिं प्रति समवायेन सिद्धेर्विरोधित्वं वाच्यम्। इत्थञ्च सिद्धिसत्त्वेऽपि विनानुमित्साम् अनुमितिः स्यात्। समवायेन ज्ञानस्य अव्याप्यवृत्तितया सिद्धिसत्त्वऽपि समवायेन तदभावस्य[22] घटाद्यवच्छेदेन सत्त्वादिति चेन्न। निरवच्छिन्नविशेषणतासम्बन्धेन सिद्ध्यभावस्य हेतुत्वात् सिद्धिसत्त्वे च तदभावस्य घटाद्यवच्छिन्नविशेषणतयैव सत्त्वान्निर्दोषः।

न च कायव्यूहस्थले एकशरीरावच्छेदेन सिद्धिसत्त्वे सिद्धिशून्यशरीरावच्छेदेनानु-मितिर्न स्यात्, निरवच्छिन्नविशेषणतया सिद्ध्यभावासत्त्वादिति वाच्यम्। एतत्शरीरावच्छिन्न-समवायेन पर्वतत्वधर्मितावच्छेदकवह्निविधेयकानुमितिं प्रति[23] समवायसम्बन्ध ावच्छिन्नप्रतियोगिताकतादृशनिश्चयाभावस्य एतत्शरीरावच्छिन्नविशषणतया हेतुत्वस्य विवक्षितत्वात्। वस्तुतस्तु अवच्छेदकतासम्बन्धेन अनुमितिं प्रति अवच्छेदकतासम्बन्ध ेन सिद्धिर्विरोधिनी, अवच्छेदकतासम्बधेन तज्ज्ञानं च व्याप्यवृत्तीति नोक्तदोषः।

(g) न चैवं परपुरुषप्रवेशस्थले[24] तत्शरीरावच्छेदेन एकात्मनि सिद्धिसत्त्वे सिद्धि-शून्यात्मनि तत्शरीरे अवच्छेदकतासम्बन्धेन अनुमितिर्न स्यात्। अवच्छेदकतासम्बन्धेन सिद्धेः तत्र सत्त्वादिति वाच्यम्। परपुरूषप्रवेशे[25] मानाभावात् भावे वा अवच्छेदकता-सम्बन्धेन एतदात्मीयानुमितिं प्रति अवच्छेदकतासम्बन्धेन एतदात्मीयसिद्धेर्विरोधितया वाच्यत्वान्न दोषः। न च महाशरीरनाशकाले सिद्धिव्युत्पादः। अनन्तरं खण्डशीरोत्पत्तिः, तत्खण्डशरीरा-वच्छेदकतासम्बन्धेन सिद्धेरभावात् विनानुमित्साम्अनुमितिः स्यादिति वाच्यम्। अवच्छेदकतासम्बन्धेन ज्ञानं प्रति शरीरस्य तादात्म्येन सहकार्यवर्तित्वेन हेतुतया शरीरनाशकाले तदवयवत्वअवच्छेदकतासम्बन्धेन ज्ञानोत्पत्तौ बाधकाभाव इति वाच्यम्। तथा सति चैत्रो जानाति इतिवत् हस्तो जानातीति प्रतीत्यापत्तेः।

(h) केचित्तु समवायसम्बन्धेन सिद्धेर्न प्रतिबन्धकत्वम्, अपितु सिद्धिविशिष्टात्म-त्वस्य। तथाच सिद्धिसत्त्वे तदभावसत्त्वेऽपि[26] सिद्धिविशिष्टात्मत्वाभावाभावात् नोक्तापत्तिसम्भवः। न च सिद्धिविशिष्टात्मत्वस्य प्रतिबन्धकत्वम् सिद्धिविशिष्टस्य[27] द्रव्यत्वादेर्वा इत्यत्र विनिगमकाभाव इति वाच्यम्। तदुभयसाधारणेन सिद्धिविशिष्टत्वेनैव प्रतिबन्धकत्वादित्याहुः। तदसत्। घटाद्यवच्छेदेन सिद्ध्य[28] भावसत्त्वे तदवच्छेदेन सिद्धिविशिष्टस्य[29] आत्मत्वसत्त्वस्यात्यन्तासम्भवितया घटाद्यवच्छेदेन सिद्ध्यभाववत्[30] सिद्धिविशिष्टात्मत्वाद्यभावस्यापि सत्त्वादुक्तापत्तेर्वारयितुमशक्यत्वमित्यास्तां विस्तरः।

(i) ननु सिषाधयिषाविरहविशिष्टसिद्ध्यभावापेक्षया बाधबुद्ध्यभावस्य लघुतया स एव पक्षता अस्तु इत्यत आह तेनेति। सिषाधयिषाविरहविशिष्टसिद्धिपरस्य[31] पक्षतास्तु तेनेत्यर्थः। साधकप्रमाणं साधकप्रमाणमेव। तथाच बाधबुद्ध्यभावविशिष्टा सिद्धिर्यत्रास्ति स न पक्ष इत्यर्थः। तस्य पक्षत्वे तत्रानुमित्यापत्तिरिति भावः। न च सिद्ध्यभावस्य[32] पक्षतात्वे यत्र सिद्ध्यभावकालीना बाधबुद्धिस्तत्रानुमितिः स्यादिति वाच्यम्। तद्विशिष्टबुद्धिं प्रति तदभावनिश्चयाभावस्य[33] हेतुतया सामान्यसामग्रीविरहादेव

तत्रापत्तिवारणात्।[34] विशिष्टान्तव्यावृत्तिंस्तेनात्र दर्शयति साधकेति। सिद्धौ सत्यामसत्यां सिषाधसिषा इत्यर्थः। तस्या[35] अपि तत्र विशिष्टाभावात् पक्षत्वमित्यनेनान्वयः। तथाच सिद्ध्यभावमात्रस्य पक्षतात्वे[36] सिषाधयिषाकालीना या सिद्धिः तत्र सिद्ध्यभावाभावात् पक्षताविरहेऽनुमितिर्न स्यात्। सिषाधयिषाविरहविशिष्टस्य[37] विशेषणत्वे तु उक्तस्थले विशेषणाभावात्[38] विशिष्टाभावसत्त्वात् पक्षतासत्त्वमिति भावः। न चात्र सिद्धिसत्त्वप्रदर्शनमेव प्रकृतमिति[39] वाच्यम्। दृष्टान्तार्थं तदुपादानात्।

(j) ननु सिषाधयिषा एव पक्षता अस्तु किं विशिष्टाभावस्य पक्षतात्वेन इत्यत आह यत्र चेति। उभयाभावः सिषाधयिषायाः सिद्धेश्च[40] अभाव इत्यर्थः। तत्र विशिष्टाभावादिति सिषाधयिषाविरहविशिष्टसिद्ध्यभावादित्यर्थः। सिषाधयिषायाः पक्षतात्वे तत्र सिषाधयिषाविरहेण पक्षताविरहेणानुमितिर्न स्यात्। सिषाधयिषाविरहविशिष्ट-सिद्ध्यभावस्य पक्षतात्वे तु विशेषणाभावकृतविशिष्टा[41] भावसत्त्वात् न पक्षताहानिरिति भावः।

चिन्तामणि-6

यद्यपि पक्षत्वस्य केवलान्वयित्वात् नास्य भेदकत्वम् तथापि पक्षपद-प्रवृत्तिनिमित्तमुक्तम्।

काणादी 6

(a) ननु लक्षणमितरभेदानुमापकम्, तथाच पक्षतालक्षणम् पक्षेतरभेदानुमापकम् वक्तव्यम्, तच्च न सम्भवति। जगत एव पक्षत्वात् इत्यत आह यद्यपीत्यादि। अस्य सिषाधयिषाविरहविशिष्टस्य भेदकत्वम् इतरभेदानुमापकत्वम्। पक्षपदप्रवृत्तिनिमित्तं पक्षपदशक्यतावच्छेदकम्। अत्र अभावार्थो[42] विवक्षितः। तेन सिद्ध्यभावस्य पक्षपद-शक्यतावच्छेदकत्वमित्यर्थः। सिद्धेः पक्षसाध्यभेदेन विभिन्नतया पक्षतावच्छेदकस्य नानात्वे पक्षपदनानार्थत्वमिति ध्येयम्। वयन्तु पक्षत्वस्य सिषाधयिषाविरहविशिष्टसिद्ध्य-भावस्य केवलान्वयित्वात् ज्ञानस्य अव्याप्यवृत्तितया सर्वत्र सत्त्वात् भेदकत्वं न सिद्धसद्व्यावृत्तकत्व[43]म्। तथाच सिद्धिसत्त्वेऽपि समवायेन सिद्ध्यभावस्य सत्त्वादनुमितिः स्यादिति भावः।

(b) समाधत्ते तथापीति। पक्षपदेति। पक्षपदोपस्थापकपर्व्वतादिपदप्रवृत्तिनिमित्त पर्व्वतत्वादिकमनिवेश्य पक्षताया हेतुत्वमिति शेषः। अयमाशयः–समवायेन अनुमितिं प्रति समवायेन सिद्धेर्न प्रतिबन्धकत्वम् येनोक्तदोषः स्यात्। अपितु वह्नित्वा-वच्छिन्नविधेयतानिरूपितविशेष्यतावच्छेदकतया अनुमितिं प्रति वाह्न्यभावत्वा-वच्छिन्नप्रकारतानिरूपितविशेष्यतावच्छेदकतया ज्ञानं प्रतिबन्धकम्। उक्तसम्बन्धेन च ज्ञानं नाव्याप्यवृत्तीति [illegible] इति ब्रूमः। पक्षताहेतुत्वव्यवस्थापनन्तु अस्माकं तर्कवादार्थमञ्जर्य्यामनुसन्धेयम् इति समाप्तोऽयं ग्रन्थः।

REFERENCES

1. This reading is supported by कणाद। रघुनाथ शिरोमणि holds the same view. There is a different reading viz. प्रमाण adopted in other texts.
2. कणाद overlooks here the other reading.

* Variant reading धर्मवत्त्वम्।

** हि is not found elsewhere.

3. Ms. reading पर्वतादिरेव
4. Ms. reading प्रतिबन्धकत्वादेरेव।
5. Ms. reading पर्व्यवह्निसंशयात् संयोगेन पर्व्वते वृक्षत्वमिति वारणाय।
6. Ms. reading सपक्षव्यावर्तकतापत्तेः।
7. Ms. reading योग्यतानुगतयोः।
8. यत्रानेकार्थोऽविवक्षितः is found in the manuscript forming the starting of the next sentence. This portion seems irrelevant and therefore the same has been kept omitted.
9. The commentary favours the reading मानम् and not प्रमाणम्।
10. Here also कणाद overlooks the other reading viz. मान।

*** Varient readings (a) स्मरणात् (b) वहुवचनस्मरणात्।

11. Ms. reading सिषाघयिषाविरहो सिद्ध मव।
12. Ms. reading इच्छाघीनत्वं प्रतिपादनार्थम्।
13. In this paragraph also कणाद completely ignores the other reading प्रमाण।
14. Ms. reading: साधकप्रमाणम् अप्रामाण्यं ज्ञानाभावविशिष्टा सिद्धिः।
15. Ms. reading: अन्यथा तस्या अपि स्वीकारात्।
16. Ms. reading: अप्रामाण्यज्ञापनाभावविशेष्यपर्वतावच्छिन्नविशेष्यतानिरुपितपर्वतत्व-व्यापकतावच्छिन्न etc.
17. Ms. reading: संयोगपर्याप्तं सांसर्गिकविषयता निरूपितवह्नित्वावच्छिन्नविधेयताकानुमितित्वेन पर्वतत्वाविशेष्यतानिरूपितपर्वतव्यापकत्वानवच्छिन्नसंयोगनिष्ठसांसर्गिकविषयतानुमितित्वेन etc.
18. Ms. reading: समानाधिकरण्यसम्बन्धतद्विशिष्टा।
19. After this word there is an insertion न प्रतिबन्धकत्वं under bracket. Perhaps this is a note indicative of the sense of the sentence.
20. Ms. reading: उभयत्व, वैशिष्ट्यसाधेयप्रागभावप्रतियोगित्वं
21. Ms. reading: निविशेष्यं किन्तु परिधायकमात्रं।

etc* तर्कवादार्थमञ्जरी is the name of another work of Kaṇāda. It is referred twice in this book, once here and again at the end. The book is not traceable now.

22. Ms. reading: तद्भावस्य।

23. Ms. reading: समवायेन सम्बन्धावच्छिन्नप्रतियोगितातादृशानिश्चयाभावस्य।
24. परपुरुषप्रवेशस्थले।
25. परपुरुषप्रवेशे।
26. तदभावसत्वे।
27. सिद्धिविशिष्टं च।
28. तदभावसत्वे।
29. सिद्धिविशिष्टं च।
30. सिद्धिभाववत्।
31. सिषाघयिषाविरहविशिष्टसिद्धिः परस्य पक्षतास्तु तेनेत्यर्थः।
32. सिद्धिभावस्य।
33. तद्भाव etc.
34. तत्रापत्तिवारणाविशिष्टान्तव्यावृत्तिंस्तुनात्र दर्शयिति।
35. तस्यापि तत्र विशिष्टापक्षत्वमित्यनेनान्वयः।
36. पक्षतात्वसिषाधयिषाकालीना सिद्धिः।
37. विशिष्टस्याविशेषणत्वे
38. विशेषणाभावत्वात्।
39. प्रकृतमिति वाच्यम्।
40. सिद्धेश्च इति भावः
41. विशिष्टाभावकृतविशिष्टाभावसत्त्वात्।
42. अत्र भावार्थो विवक्षितः।
43. सिद्धसद्व्यावर्तकत्वम् is a better reading here.

Index of References

(*Pakṣatācintāmaṇī*)

Pakṣatācintāmaṇī Kāṇādī

English Translation

Pakṣatācintāmaṇi-I

Next to व्याप्ति (pervasion of the probandum in the probans), पक्षधर्मता (state of being the qualification of the subject of inference) is being described. There the subject-essence in respect to inference is not to be taken as the state of being the attribute of the probandum put to doubt. Doubt in no way can be the attribute, for, it perishes before the stage of परामर्श (stage of synthetic confirmation) with the advent of perception of the mark, recollection of universal concomitance etc. Nor it can be taken as an indication. For, then its nature of being the differentiating factor will be put to question. Even negation of supporting and contradicting evidences cannot be the attribute. For, negation of both remains continuing even if each of its constituents happens to be present. In the same way, two negations cannot be the attribute. Because, in that case, negation of contradicting evidence will be liable to futility. And even when lakes etc. are taken as subjects, inferential knowledge does not arise owing to invariable consideration of fallacy of inconsistency, lack of foundation of the probans etc.

Kāṇādī-I

(a) Salutation to गणेश (God of success). About the text व्याप्ति etc. Next to व्याप्ति means next to description of व्याप्ति. The term पक्षधर्मता may be analysed either as पक्षे धर्मता यस्य or as पक्षरूपो यो धर्मस्तस्य भाव: yielding the sense that what is described is पक्षता i.e. subject-essence in inferential proposition. Thus it becomes a different topic by the description of पक्षता. In accordance with relevance of performing the same act in the form of inferential process, the author in order to describe subject-essence of inference makes proposition to the students to arouse their alertness. To inform means a function conducive to knowledge in the form of application of sentence. Here the word व्याप्ति is to be taken in the secondary sense of description of व्याप्ति. The term अनन्तर means the act of following arising out of causation of destruction etc. And to its partial meaning destruction, description of व्याप्ति i.e. the meaning conveyed by the term व्याप्ति is related in the relation of counterpositiveness. The meaning of the root is objectness. Objectness again belongs to them who are connected with the functional part. Therefore, no damage occurs even if a word does not contain object-essence. And sentential meaning becomes constructed in this way—sunject-essence is the object of description of the act of following arising out of instrumentality of destruction in respect to description of व्याप्ति. The seventh case-ending in the word निरूपण denotes objectness. And that has syntactical relation to पक्षत्वम् i.e. subject-essence in inferential proposition.

(b) About the text सन्दिग्ध etc. According to the derivation सन्दिग्धः साध्यरूपो धर्म्मो यस्य (whose character in the form of the probandum is doubtful) the term सन्दिग्धसाध्यधर्मवत्त्व precisely taken as सन्दिग्ध साध्यवत्त्वधर्मवत्त्व conveys the meaning of locatedness delimited by the relation of the determinant of probandumness and more precisely, of doubtful in the probandum. That (doubtful) in relation of identity may imply alternatively the meaning of subjectessence in inferential proposition. Indeed, in the instance of (inferable) fire etc. locatedness delimited by conjunct relation and described by mountain etc. happens to be doubtful, and for this reason subject-essence falls upon mountain etc. in relation of identity. It is not the case that ascertainment of the pervaded also is expressed in the statement. Because, firstly in (the instance of) inference containing past and future fire as predicative there will occur the situation of absence of subject-essence on the strength of the ground that immediately before inference there will be non-existence of the qualification of being container of doubtful-fire etc. in the location of mountain and so on. Secondly there will occur the situation of absence of subject-essence in (the instance of) inference constituted of subject past and future. Also where ether in intimate relation will be the inferable property in the location of darkness there will arise the question of non-existence of subject-essence. Because, locatedness delimited by the relation of inherence determined by darkness is not real. Even what the author says about doubtness in respect of probandum constituting subjectness is not correct, for it is impossible to speak of one common essence of doubt in respect of probandum which is uniformly present in the situations of probandum once forming the subjective and elsewhere forming the character. Because the import lies in the fact that subject-essence of inference is that sort of cognition which penetrates both subject and probandum and which becomes obstructed by confirmative knowledge formed of the subject as substantive and the probandum as character. And this becomes evident in the case of doubt in the form 'where the mountain is fiery or not' or in the form 'whether there is fire or not in the mountain' or in the form of both taken together, all becoming obstructed by the confirmative knowledge 'the mountain contains fire'. The essence of subjectness belongs to both of them constituted of what accomodates the characteristic of both fire and mountain. But the confirmative knowledge of mountain possessed of fire accomodates within itself the characteristic of both mountain and fire. And as such, in order to avoid alleged imposition of the essence of subjectness upon it the portion upto प्रतिबध्यम्(i.e. पक्षविशेष्यकसाध्यप्रकारकनिश्चयप्रतिबध्यम्) in the text above has been incorporated.

(c) Again subjectness becomes allegedly due also to the confimative knowledge of contradiction in the form 'the mountain contains absence of fire' on the ground that it is an object of obstruction by the ascertainment constitued of mountain as substantive and fire as charcter. That is why the substantive (i.e. पक्षसाध्योभयावगाहिज्ञानम्) has been mentioned as such. It is not the case that there is no harm in accepting the ascertainment of contradiction as possessing of the essence of subjectness. And this cannot be supported further by the supposition that in spite of subjectness belonging to ascertainment of contradiction the allegation of emergence of inferential knowledge can be repudiated on the strength of argument that confirmation of contradiction contains property of the obstructor towards inference. Only ascertainment of contradiction unattacked by knowledge of invalidity is opposed to inference. And therefore, where there is ascertainment of contradiction attacked by knowledge of invalidity it becomes very difficult there to counteract the logic of emergence of inference. Because presence of subjectness in the form of ascertainment of contradiction is there and there is presence also of negation of ascertainment unattacked by knowledge of invalidity.

(d) Here again for want of one single probandumness etc. subjectness should be spoken of as specified. Thus essence of subjectness in respect of inferential cognition which takes shape out of predicative delimited by fireness and which again is determined by relational objectness present in conjunction and by substantiveness delimited by the attribute of mountainness is but essence of knowledge formed of object delimited by fireness and determined by the objectness delimited by mountainness and which is covered at the same time by a condition that this (knowledge) contains the state of being obstructed by such ascertainment whose character is delimited by fireness and which is determined by relational objectness present in conjunction and which is determined by the substantiveness delimited by mountainness. Relational objectness present in conjunction is incorporated here only to exclude such cases as fireness in the location of mountain in conjunct relation alleged to be originated out of doubt about fire related to mountain in inherent relation.

(e) The author in his text सन्देहो हि etc. is demonstrating defects of what is covered by the language-expression heard so far. With the aid of perception of mark, recollection of pervasion etc, that is to say, by any one of the perception of mark, recollection of pervasion etc. Because of destruction of that doubt. Where perception of mark occurs first, then occurs recollection of pervasion and after that occurs synthetic confirmation doubt becomes destroyed there due to perception of mark. Where again recollection of pervasion occurs first, then occurs mark-perception, doubt ceases there with the recollection of pervasion. And thus probandum qualified by doubt does not exist prior to emergence of inference and therefore that cannot possess the essence of subjectness.

(f) It may be aruged that if the essence of location of the probandum being an object of doubt at any time be accepted as subjectness then there will arise no fault mentioned above. Anticipating this the author refutes the argument by saying that it is not even an indicator. Because, if it be so there will be objection of its being non-differentiating attribute, i.e. the attribute which does not help in producing differentiation from similar instance (सपक्ष). Thus for example, the objection of emergence of inference in the form "the mountain is fiery' becomes inevitable even if there remains confirmation that the mountain is fiery on the strength of the ground that the mountain still at that time possesses the essence of location of fire taken to be an object of doubt at any time. Conclusive definition to this effect completely loses ground owing to the fact that doubt becomes destroyed prior to synthetic confirmation. Even only capacity of being an object of doubt cannot be subject-essence. It cannot be favoured with the argument that capacity of being doubtful may remain even when doubt does not exist at all thereby leaving no scope of the fault spoken of above. Because, capacity and homogeneous attribute, none can be identified in isolation.

(g) The author criticises definition of someone else in नापि etc. The text साधक etc. मानम् means मिति i.e. cognition. It is to be taken in the sense of being uninvaded by the knowledge of invalidity. Thus what subjectness means is the negation of ascertainment of inconsistency and foundation uninvaded by knowledge of invalidity. It is not to be argued that in cases of exclusively affirmative inferential property confirmation of inconsistency is not possible due to absurdity of negation of the probandum, for in the case of negation existing in a pot there may arise ascertainment of inconsistency in the form 'pot is not denotative' caused by the erratic understanding of denotativeness as negatumness.

(h) It may be supposed that negation relating to foundation and confirmation of inconsistency will possess the attribute of probans either in the form of locus-essence of negation described by the essence of negatum delimited by bothness belonging to foundation (of inferable property) and confirmation of inconsistency, or in the form of property of negation of the unfounded or that of negation concerning confirmation of inconsistency. To this the author is criticising the first alternative in the text उभयाभावस्य etc. i.e. relating to negation of both taken together etc. This means relating to negation described by essence of negatum delimited by bothness of foundation of confirmation of inconsistency. Because, in spite of existence of each i.e., in spite of existence of even one between foundation and confirmation of inconsistency, that happens to exist. Thus the significance is that there will be objection of having no bar in the origination of inferential knowledge in a situation where there is simultaneously negation of inconsistency and foundation of inferable property or confirmation of inconsistency and negation of foundation. The author criticises the second alternative by the text नापि etc. Two negations refer to negation of foundation and negation of inconsistency. The text with reference to negation of contradictory evidence means to have reference of confirmation of inconsistency uninvaded by knowledge of invalidity.

(i) Now, if only negation of foundation be accepted as the property of subject-essence, a question may be asked as to why there will not arise inference in the form 'the lake is fiery' in a situation where confirmatin of inconsistency remains in the form 'the lake is devoid of fire.' To this, the author says ह्रदादे: etc. Explanation refers to

बाधहेत्वसिद्ध्यादे: etc. Inconsistency means confirmation of inconsistency. Non-existence of foundation of the probans refers fo knowledge of not being located in the subject in respect of the probans. By virtue of the term आदि fallacy of counterbalance (i.e. सत्प्रतिपक्ष) becomes included. By dint of essential factor means by dint of invariably fixed co-relator in respect of non-origination of inferential cognition. Because of non-origination of inference implies because of allegation in respect of emergence of inference being possible to be refuted. And the resultant implication is that there will be no harm in acknowledging mere negation of foundation as the attribute of subject-essence in inferential proposition.

Pakṣatācintāmaṇi-2

It is not even negation of supporting evidence; because, in the Vedic Sentence श्रेतव्यो मन्तव्य: etc. there is indication of inferential judgement occurring after auditory perception of the same content, because inference is seen to be originated even on an object already perceived by senses, because an object known by one reason happens to be known by another reason also, and because there is authority of the Scriptural sentence 'मन्तव्यश्चोपपत्तिभि:' i.e. should be judged by several reasons.

Kāṇādī-2

(a) A question may be asked—if mere non-existence of foundation is thus declared subjectness what for is the further attempt of determining it? To this question, the author remarks नापि etc. Negation of supporting evidence means negation of foundation unattacked by knowledge of invalidity. श्रोतव्यो मन्तव्य: etc. refers to the instrumentality of the Vedic injunction 'आत्मा वाऽरे श्रोतव्यो मन्तव्यो निदिध्यासितव्य:। आत्मा साक्षात् द्रष्टव्य:', समानविषयक etc. means after occurence of authoritative knowledge of Self, मननवोधनात् means because of inferential knowledge formed of Self as content. It follows therefore that there may not arise inferential knowledge due to non-existence of negation of foundation as there already exists foundation in the form of authoritative knowledge.

(b) Now if it is argued that let mere negation of perceptual foundation be decleared subjectness and there will be no such fault as spoken above, the author goes on answering प्रत्यक्ष etc. Because, in spite of the existence of perceptual foundation inference is seen to be originated out of inferential will. And under the condition inferential cognition sould not have arisen there due to non-existence of negation of foundation. But some scholars explain the Vedic injunction श्रोतव्य: etc., as conveying the sense of inference occuring simply after verbal cognition and not immediately after verbal cognition and that inferential judgement (taken in that sense) may occur even after verbal cognition. That is why the author mentions another defect प्रत्यक्षदृष्टेऽपि etc. This has been explained already—those scholars say.

(c) Again, let negation only of foundation in the form of inferential cognition be declared subjectness and there will arise no scope of the aforesaid fault. Assuming this the author goes on saying एकलिङ्ग etc. In the case of having one reason means inspite of the existence of its inferential cognition. Because of inference means because of the origination of its inferential cognition. If it is aruged that once inference is produced by one reason inference by another reason is unfounded, the author replies मन्तव्यश्च etc.. मन्तव्य: means to be judged by inference and उपपत्तिभि: denotes by various reasons. Though the meaning of the śāstric injunction मन्तव्य: etc., may be carried out successfully even in the case of inference arising out of a different reason occuring after cessation of inference originated by another reason, yet fault should be observed lying here in this way : where inference produced by one reason already exists and then arises question of inference by a different reason no inference can emerge there successfully due to non-existence of negation of foundation in the form of inference. Again, if negation of inference having fire as its predicative, mountainness as its limitor of qualificandness and smoke as its mark be considered as defining characteristic of subjectness in such inference whose predicative is fire, limitor of qualificandness is mountainness and whose mark is smoke there will be no scope of fault spoken above due to the advantage of procedure adopted in formulating subjectness. This argument does not stand criticism. Because, where there is such intention as—let there emerge dual inference and emergence of dual inference follows there in consequence after occurrence of confirmation of mountain having conjunction of smoke pervaded by fire, the emergence of inference second in order will be put to objection there. Because, this inference also contains attribute of such inference whose predicative, is fire, limitor of qualificandness is mountainness and mark is smoke and prior to emergence of that inference there does not remain non-existence of negation of inference having fire as its predicative, mountainness as its limitor of qualificandness and smoke as its mark.

Pakṣatācintāmaṇi-3

Now, let it be supposed that subject of inferential proposition is that qualificand which contains probandum intended to be established as its qualification. Thus for example, it spite of cognition of self acquired from Scriptures one desirous of deliverance takes recourse to inference of self out of aspiration for inferential judgement in respect to specific foundation guided by the principle that absorption in inferential judgement is the way to salvation. Contradiction, therefore, does not rest between these two comments of Vācaspati—(1) Those who are fond of inferrential judgement want to enjoy through inference objects even when they are grasped by perception. (2) Agents of inference do not apply inference to know an elephant by roaring sound when that is already visualised by senses.

Kāṇādī-3

सिषाधयिषिता etc. Subjectness means attribute of the support of the probandum being the object of will for inference. It cannot be argued that there will be occurrance of deviation in the case of inference composed of predicative past and future, due to prior negation of the probandum forming the object of will for inference. Because significance lies in the expectancy of will for foundation of the probandum. And therefore, as there is no single homogeneous property belonging to probandumness etc. subjectness having fire as its predicative and mountainness as its limitor of qualificandness means will for inference with fire as its predicative and mountainness as its limitor of qualificandness and subjectness should be defined as such. The author is demonstrating fitness of the definition in the definables in the text तथाहि etc. सिद्धिविशेषे etc. This means due to that will whose object is specific foundation in the form of inference. एतएव etc. Just becasue of causality of inference belonging to will for establishment. तदुपपत्ते: means due to solution of contradiction belonging to those two sentences.

Pakṣatācintāmaṇi-4

Nor can it be argued that origination of inference can be accounted for by inferential will and its negation. Because, just like the position of doubt inferential will also does not exist before synthetic confirmation. Capacity of being an object of the inferential will is not possible to be determined. Even in the case of non-existence of inferential will there arises inferential cognition as in the case of

inference of cloud by dint of thunder-sound. And inference of unscheduled character also is seen to have emerged out of thirdtime consideration of the mark included in its own group of causes.

Kāṇādī-4

(a) The term सन्देहवत् means like the position of doubt. सिसाधयिषाया अपि i.e. even of will of establishment, and that with the aid of recollection of pervasion etc., it means. Because of negation means because of destruction. Thus it is implied that causal efficiency does not belong to inferential will due to violation. And in order to counteract the supposition that there will arise another inferential will resulting in therefrom further inferential cognition the author states सिषाधयिषाविरहेऽपि etc. In spite of nonexistence of will for inference of cloud—it is meant here. Because of inference of cloud caused by that specific type of sound. The meaning is that because of inference like 'this time is related to cloud because of its qualification of the support of sound of specific character.' It may be argued from the critic's point of view that even in that case there is no bar as to the originatin of inferential will and therefore non-existence of will for inference is unfounded. To this the author replies स्वकारणाधीन etc. The word स्वं refers to third consideration of the mark. It is included in the same cluster of causes to which recollection of pervasion etc. belongs. This is the significance.

(b) A critic may ask 'speak simply परामर्शबलेन (by force of synthetic confirmation) and what is the use of uttering स्वकारणाधीनत्व (qualification of coming under its own group of causes)? A reply should be made to this effect.' The reason as stated is that mention has been made of that in order to establish inclusiveness of synthetic confirmation into will. As there is inclusiveness of synthetic confirmation into will inferential will is supposed to contain element of necessity there. Because, will for the end is the cause of will for the means. अनपेक्षित etc. It means, as inference is seen to be produced on being confirmed as dependent upon will. Thus where there is confirmation that inference is not a desired measure there cannot arise will for inferential cognition. But emergence of inference is proved there by experience. Hence due to deviation causality cannot be attributed to will for establishment.

Pakṣatācintāmaṇi-5

It is being concluded. Inferential subject is that which contains non-existence of supporting evidence together with non-existence of inferential will. Therefore, what contains supporting evidence together with non-existence of inferential will cannot be termed

subject. Where there is inferential will irrespective of presence or absence of supporting evidence, or, where there is negation of both, there remains qualification of inferential subject due to presence of qualified negation.

Kāṇādī-5

(a) सिषाधयिषाविरहविशिष्ट etc. Negation of that supporting evidence which is qualified by negation of inferential will is what is meant by subjectness. Will for establishment is will for inference. साधकप्रमाणम् means foundation qualified by negation of knowledge of invalidity, foundation not in respect of effect, for that is not intended by the author. The formation of the word प्रमाण as it stands for प्रमिति (knowldege) due to its derivation in the root-sense finds justification in the sense of getting the state of being unattacked by the knowledge of invalidity. Ascertainment of probandum taken as limitor of probandumness should be understood as occurring in the subject taken as limitor of subjectness. Where there is ascertainment as 'stone-made location contains fire' there occurs inference in the form 'the mountain contains fire' even without any will for establishment and that is why limitor of subjectness has been incorporated. Likewise in spite of non-existence of will for establishment where there already exists ascertainment as 'the mountain is illuminating' there occurs inferential cognition as 'the mountain is fiery' and for this reason limitor of probandumness has been incorporated. And where there is existence of foundation in one relation, inference occurs there in another relation even without any will for inference and as such incorporation of relation also becomes necessary. In a situation where there is will for establishment at first and then occurs multiqualificand synthetic confirmation (समूहालम्बनपरामर्श) like 'the mountain contains fire and the mountain contains something pervaded by fire' and inferential cognition originates therefrom there is lack of negation of foundation and in order to create opportunity of subjectness there the portion of the text ending in विशिष्ट (qualified) has been added to सिद्धि (foundation) as qualification. And thus due to existence of qualified negation made up of negation of adjective in the form of non-existence of will for establishment there remains existence of subjectness.

(b) A critic may argue that foundation being present inference may take place even from such will as 'let there arise knowledge manifesting merely something, becasue that will also possess the nature of will containing inference as content. It cannot be said that will characterised by the nature of inference only will be the stimulator, for even from will in the form 'let there generate cognition other than perception,' inference takes rise out of synthetic confirmation in the form of foundation. This sort of argument is not tenable. Because causality as intended here is in the form of negation of foundation qualified by heaps of negations pertaining to those wills of specific character and to foundation which when present produces inferential cognition. Again objection cannot be raised to too many cause and effect relations taking advantage of the ground that there is no criterion of forming mutually subjctive and adjective relations among heaps of negations of certain specific character. Because that will have to be acknowledged otherwise also.

(c) Here again subjectness should be defined as qualified, because of non-existence of homogeneity among attributes of subject. And thus as in inferential knowledge whose predicative is limited by what is determined by substantiveness limited by mountainness and by relational objectness present in conjunction inferrential subject qualified by mass of negations in respect of all wills happens to be vitiated by invalidity, subjectness is defined as non-existence of confirmative knowledge determined by the character-essence limited by fireness and by the substantive-essence limited by mountainness and by mass of negations. Also in similar cases elsewhere where there is ascertainment as 'the mountain contains fire' there may arise inferential cognition in such a form as 'the fiery mountain is a substance' even without any aid of will for establishment. In order to check deviation of the definition in such cases predicative-essence has been incorporated in the definition in lieu of character-essence. And as fire does not possess predicative-essence, defect of deviation has been avoided there. Predicative-essence is a kind of character-essence witnessed by the introspective knowledge such as 'I infer'.

(d) Here again without any aid of will for inference inferential cognition happens to take place in the form 'the mountain contains fire' in spatial limit of the delimitor even though there exists already ascertainment as 'the mountain is fiery' in relation of co-presence determined by mountainness. And for this reason foundation in relation of special limit of delimitor should be counted as attribute of obstructor in respect to inference in relation of spatial limit of delimitor. And determined by limitor of subjectness means the essence of pervader of delimitor of subjectness and that appears there in the character without having any relation even. Towards inference in relation of co-existence of its own determinant foundation in relation of co-existence of limitor of subject-essence and in relation of spacial limit of limitor of subject-essence becomes obstructor. Inference in relation of co-existence of limitor of subjectessence however may otherwise be known as inference determined by relational objectness covered adequately by conjunction etc. It follows therefore that obstructedness becomes constructed in the form of inference-essence whose predicativeness is limited by fireness and which is determined by the relational objectessence present in conjunction limited by nonpervaderness in relation to mountainness and which again is described by the objectness limited by mountainness. And obstructorness becomes constructed as the essence of ascertainment whose qualifierness is limited by fireness and which is determined by relational objectness present in conjunction and limited by non-pervaderness in relation to mountainness and determined by the substantive-essence limited by mountainness and qualified by negation of knowledge of invalidity and further qualified by nonexistence of will for establishment. Here again inference in spatial limit of limitor may otherwise be understood as stimulator. And hence obstructedness may be understood either as property of inference whose predicativeness is limited by fireness described by relational objectness extended totally in conjunction and determined by substantiveness limited by mountainness or as property of inference whose relational objectness exists in conjunction not limited by pervader-essence in relation to mountain-essence and which determined by the substantiveness limited by mountainness. Relation of the obstructed and the obstructor should be understood in this way.

(e) Foundation remaining existing those varieties of will which while present yield inferential knowledge, conglomeration of their non-existence should not be incorporated in the side of limitor of obstructorness. But incorporation should be made only of general nonexistence of will which in relation of co-existence is qualified by effort which again is qualified by inference not containing fire as predicative, fire the limitor of qualificandness in respect to mountainness in relation of both co-existence and denotativeness of its own prior non-existence. There being foundation as 'the mountain contains fire' all such types of will which while present generate inference as 'the mountain contains fire' bear possessiveness of the aforesaid generic attribute— according to the Neo-Ligicians. However, the fact is that in the instance of inference other than qualified by foundation foundation-essence plays the part of obstructor-essence, while in inference arising out of will for establishment causality goes to will for establishment. Bothness implies qualification in relation of both of co-existence and counter-positiveness of prior non-existence of the located itself. There again selfness should not be placed by limitor of relation-essence but should be counted simply as indicator. Because, counterpositiveness of prior non-existence of what is located in one locus does not possess essence of another relation. However, details may be found in our तर्कवादार्थमञ्जरी.

(f) From the critic's point of view it may be argued thus: Let foundation in inherence be deemed as possessing contradictoriness towards inference in inherence. And even when foundation exists inference may be produced without any aid of will for inference under this condition. Because, knowledge in inherence has partial extension and in spite of existence of foundation its non-existence in inherence in the spatial limit of pot etc. remains continuing. This agrument is futile. Because, non-existence of foundation contains causality only in relation of unlimited adjectivity (निरवच्छिन्न-विशेषणता) and therefore where foundation exists, its non-existence remains there only as adjectivity limited by pot etc. and no question of fault arises. It cannot be argued that in the case of कायव्यूह (one soul assuming more than one body-frame by dint of special power achieved through performance of योग or meditation) there being foundation in spatial limit of one body inference cannot be accepted in the spatial limit of other body devoid of foundation on the plea that since adjectivity is spoken of having no limit negation of foundation cannot continue there. Because, towards inference in inherence limited by this particular body containing fire as predicative and mountainness as delimitor of qualificandness causality relating to non-existence of that sort of ascertainment whose counterpositiveness is limited by inherent relation is intended in the from of adjectivity limited by this particular body. However, the fact is that foundation in relation of delimitorness is contradictory to inference in relation of delimitorness and that knowledge in relation of delimitorness covers a whole area and thus no question of fault mentioned above arises.

(g) Again, it would be wrong to make such objection that in the case of soul entering another body (reference of कायव्यूह continues) there being foundation in one abode of soul in the spatial limit of that particular body inference may not take place in relation of delimitorness in another body above devoid of foundation on the plea of argument that foundation exists there in relation of delimitorness. The reason is that there is no such evidence in support of entrance (of soul) into another frame of body. Or if it is taken for granted that it is a fact it may be explained thus: Towards inference of this particular soul in relation of delimitorness foundation in respect to this particular soul in relation of delimitorness is contradictory. Thus there is no question of problem. Again there may be counter-argument: At the time of destruction of gross body foundation loses existence. Partial body emerges afterwards. Foundation does not exist in that partial body in relation of delimitorness, and there arises ground of inference without any aid of will for inference. This counter-argument is not maintainable. It cannot be adduced in support of this counter-argument that since in respect of knowledge in relation of delimitorness bodyframe contains causality due to its co-presence in the same effect in relation of identity there is no bar as to the origination of knowledge at the time of destruction of body in relation of delimitorness of essence of its parts. Because, in that situation just like 'Caitra is knowing' cognition in the form 'the hand is knowing' may be alleged to have occurrence.

(h) Some other logicians put arguments in this way: Obstructorness belongs not to foundation in relation of inherence but to soul-essence qualified by foundation. And thus in presence of foundation and even in absence of foundation there remains no negation of soul-essence qualified by foundation and as a result there occurs no scope of the aforesaid problem. It cannot be advocated that there is no criterion of determining obstructorness in this way—whether it belongs to soul-essence qualified by foundation or to substance-essence and the like qualified by foundation. Because obstructorness is by nature the state of being qualified by foundation, the common state of both of them. This argument does not hold good. Because when there exists negation of foundation in spatial limit of pot and the like, existence of soul-essence qualified by foundation in spatial limit of that becomes quite impossible. And just like negation of foundation in spatial limit of pot and the like negation also of soul-essence and the like qualified by foundation happens to continue and therefore problem raised earlier becomes difficult to be overcome. Let this much be sufficient without detailing further.

(i) If it is argued that negation of cognition of inconsistency (बाधबुद्धि) is lighter than negation of foundation qualified by absence of will for establishment in comparison and therefore let that be declared as subjectness, the author goes on saying तेन etc. Let subjectness stand for foundation qualified by absence of will for establishment. तेन means what follows therefore. साधकप्रमाणं means supporting evidence only. And thus it is denoted that what contains fundation qualified by negation of knowledge of inconsistency is not subject of inferential proposition. The idea is that if subjectness to that effect becomes accepted there will arise the allegation of acknowledging inference. Again it cannot be a point that if non-existence of foundation be acknowledged defining characteristic of subject then where there is knowledge of inconsistency contemporaneous of negation of foundation inference may come into existence there. Because, causality directed towards knowledge qualified by particulat that pertains to non-existence of ascertainment of negation of particular that and therefore allegation becomes avoided there simply due to nonexistence of totality of causes in general. That is why the author is showing in the text साधक etc. utility in terms of non-application of the sentence ending in विशिष्ट. Will for establishment irrespective of presence or absence of foundation. That again is related to the विशिष्टाभावात् पक्षत्वम्. In this way if only negation of foundation be regarded as containing essence of subjectness then where there is foundation contemporaneous of will for establishment there is ground of non-exiestence of subjectness owing to non-existence of negation of foundation, and inference may not come into being there. But if the state qualified by negation of will for establishment be considered as adjective then in the above instance due to existence of qualified negation by virtue of negation of adjective subjectness remains continuing there—it means. It will be unjust to say that demonstration of existence of foundation only is the actual intention here, for that has been taken into account for the purpose of illustration.

(j) Let only will for establishment be considered as subjectness, what's the use of declaring qualified negation as containing essence of subjectness? To this the author replies यत्र च etc. Negaion of both means negation of will for establishment and negation of foundation. विशिष्टाभावात् in the text means due to non-existence of foundation qualified by negation of will for establishment. If essence of subjectness pertains to will for establishment then subjectness falls short there owing to non-existence of will for establishment and resulting in non-appearance of inference. But if essence of subjectness belongs to negation of foundation qualified by negation of will for establishment then subjectness does not fall short because of existence of qualified negation framed of negation of adjective. This is the import.

Pakṣatācintāmaṇi-6

Though subjectness (पक्षात्व) does not contain attribute of differentiator due to its exclusive affirmative character, yet it is mentioned as the cause of use of the term पक्ष.

Kāṇādī-6

(a) It may be argued that definition is the criterion of differentiation from other than definables, and therefore, definition of subjectness should be stated as the measure of differentiation from whatever is other than the subject, and that is not possible in as-much as all world contains the essence of subject. In order to defend such attack the author goes on saying यद्यपि etc. The term अस्य refers to the state qualified by negation of will for establishment. भेदकत्वम् means essence of measure of differentiation from other than definables. पक्षपदप्रवृत्तिनिमित्त (reason for use of the term पक्ष) is expressive of delimitor of essence of what is denoted by the term पक्ष. Here it is intended in the sense of negation. It implies therefore, that essence of delimitor in respect to essence of what is denoted by the term पक्ष pertains to non-existence of foundation. It should be noted that foundation differs in respect of difference of subject and probandum resulting in varieties of delimitor of subjectness and makes room for varieties of meaning of the term पक्ष. We, however, are of opinion that as subjectness in the form of negation of foundation qualified by non-existence of will for establishment is of exclusively affirmative character and as knowledge is characterised by partial extension everywhere, essence of differentiator should not be considered as containing the notion of being differentiated by what is fixed as affirmative (सिद्धसद्व्यावृत्तकत्वम्). And thus it is clear that even in the case of existence of foundation, non existence of the same may exist in inherence and this paves the way for emergence of inference.

(b) The author makes solution by तथापि etc. Explanation in respect of पक्षपद etc. The clarified meaning is that causality has been mentioned of पक्षता instead of mentioning पर्व्वत etc. the reason for the use of the term पर्व्वत etc. which is representative of the term पक्ष. The significance is as follows: foundation in inherence does not contain obstructor-essence towards inference in inherence. Failure of this condition might have created the said fault. Moreover, towards inference helped by limitor-essence of substantiveness determined by predicativeness limited by fireness knowledge helped by limitor-essence of substantiveness determined by character-essence limited by fireness and (at the same time) determined by character-essence limited by contra-existentiality of fire is the obstructor. And in the said relation knowledge cannot be marked as containing partial extension and no question of the said fault arises in such explanation, we contend. Critical explanation in respect to causality contained in subjectness may be found in our तर्कवादार्थमञ्जरी. Here ends the work.

[Synopsis: Relevance of discussion on subjectness of inferential proposition, probable definition of subjectness with doubt as a constituent, faults of the definition shown, definition rejected, another faulty definition of the same comprising negation of supporting and contradicting knowledge shown and rejected, nonexistence of foundation as a probable definition proved to be faulty and rejected, conclusive definition of subjectness established. Subject-essence (पक्षता) not the differentiating attribute, but still the cause of the use of the term पक्ष. The commentator discusses at length different aspects of definitions rejected, conclusive definition of subjectness in general and that of subjectness in particular, the theory of the obstructor and the obstructed, theory of the stimulator, nature of obstruction in particular instances, problem of the conclusive definition in the case of कायव्यूह i.e., one soul assuming many body-forms, faulty explanation of other legicians on some points etc.]

Part II

Sāmānyanirukti of Gaṅgeśa

with

Kaṇādaṭippaṇī

Mūla, Ṭippaṇī & English translation

Editorial Note

The topic known as general definition of *Hetvābhāsa* (feigned reason) in Gaṅgeśa's *Tattvacintāmaṇi* (*Anumānakhaṇḍa*) goes by the name *Sāmānyanirukti* in Navya-Nyāya Literature. Gaṅgeśa speaks of five varieties of *Hetvābhāsa* i.e. *Savyabhicāra, Viruddha, Satpratipakṣa, Asiddha* and *Bādhita* and elaborates their defining attributes with ample illustrations and mentions their way of vitiating the emergence of inferential cognition. But before going to that specific analysis he makes an attempt to formulate a general definition of *Hetvābhāsa* proper the nature of which belongs to each of the five individual faulty reasons. This is a difficult task and he formulates three such definitions to suit the general characteristics of feigned reason and the commentators took liberty to explain those definitions in their own way to show their individual proficiency in the subject and logical acumen of their own to invent problematic conditions and at the same time their probable solutions too in order to prove those definitions all the more accurate and perfect.

The present text is constructed from two manuscripts of *Kaṇādaṭippanī* on *Anumānacintāmaṇi* available in the collections of the Asiatic Society, Kolkata (Vide-Descriptive Catalogue of the Sanskrit Manuscripts, Government Collections, Vol XI, No. 7604/3504 and 7605/785). The first copy containing 188 folios is shown as complete in the catalogue. But on scrutiny it is detected that several chapters are missing or omitted in the text. The Pakṣatā-section for example is an illustration of that gap. The condition of the manuscript is not good and in many places it is very difficult to understand and trace the actual writing of the scribe. The second copy consists of fragments only. The text of *Sāmānyanirukti* is available in both the copies. For the purpose of text construction the first copy (i.e. 7604/3504) has been utilised as the base material and the second copy for correcting lacuna etc.

At the very beginning of the first copy there is the following Śloka that contains the name of the author as Kaṇāda. Cf.—

सार्वभौमपदाम्भोजभ्रमरीकृतमौलिना।
अनुमानाख्यमणिव्याख्या श्रीकणादेन तन्यते।।

सामान्यनिरुक्तिः

(चिन्तामणौ हेत्वाभासनिरूपणम्[1])

1. अथ हेत्वाभासास्तत्त्वनिर्णय-विजयप्रयोजकत्वान्निरूप्यन्ते।
2. ततानुमितिकारणीभूताभावप्रतियोगियथार्थज्ञानविषयत्वं, यद्विषयत्वेन लिङ्गज्ञानस्यानुमितिप्रतिबन्धकत्वं,[2] ज्ञायमानं सदनुमितिप्रतिबन्धकत्वं यत् तत्त्वं वा हेत्वाभासत्वम्।
3. दशाविशेषे हेत्वोरेवासाधारणसत्प्रतिपक्षयोराभासत्वात्तद्बुद्धेरप्य-नुमितिप्रतिबन्धकत्वम्।
4. यद्यपि बाध-सत्प्रतिपक्षयोः प्रत्यक्षशाब्दज्ञानप्रतिबन्धकत्वान्न लिङ्गाभासत्वं तथापि ज्ञायमानस्याभासस्यात्र लक्षणम्।
5. यद् वा प्रत्यक्षादौ बाधेन न ज्ञानं प्रतिबध्यते किन्तूत्पन्नज्ञानेऽप्रामाण्यं ज्ञाप्यते अनुमितौ तूत्पत्तिरेव प्रतिबध्यते। ते च सव्यभिचार-विरुद्ध-सत्प्रतिक्षासिद्धबाधिताः पञ्च।

   इति श्रीमद्गङ्गेशोपाध्यायविरचिते तत्त्वचिन्तामणौ अनुमानाख्य-द्वितीयखण्डे हेत्वाभासे हेत्वाभाससामान्यनिरुक्तिः।[3]

॥ कणादकृता सामान्यनिरुक्तिटिप्पनी ॥

[1]विचिन्त्य दूर्वादलवर्णशोभापादप्रफुल्लोत्पलरेणुमन्तम्[2]।
तनोति यत्नेन कणादनामा चिन्तामणेश्चिन्तितगूढमर्थम्।।[3]

(हेत्वाभासनिरूपणे प्रयोजनम्)

1. **अथेति।** व्याप्त्यादिसहितहेतुनिरूपणानन्तरमित्यर्थः। **हेत्वाभासाः** हेतुदोषाः। तत्त्वनिर्णयेति। प्रमाणतत्त्वनिर्णयवादिविजययोः प्रयोजकत्वादित्यर्थः। स्वहेतोः सद्धेतुत्वव्यवस्थापने प्रतिवादिहेतोराभासत्वव्यवस्थापने[4] तत्त्वनिर्णयादिसम्भवादिति भावः। तथाच[5] एककार्यकारित्वसङ्गत्या हेत्वाभासनिरूपणमित्यर्थः।[6] न चैवं धूमादीनामपि निरूपणप्रसङ्गः। तस्य वादिविजयप्रयोजकत्वेऽपि तत्त्वनिर्णयानुपयोगित्वात्। न चैवमपि तत्त्वनिर्णयोपयोगितया न्यूनाधिकाप[7] सिद्धान्तानां निरूपणमेव किमिति न कृतमिति वाच्यम्। स्वतन्त्रेच्छाया इत्यादि न्यायात् हेतुना विरोधादिसम्बन्धेन स्मृतस्य हेत्वाभासस्य उपेक्षानर्हत्वात्। प्रसङ्गसङ्गतिरपि[8] द्रष्टव्या। **निरूप्यन्ते** लक्षणस्वरूपप्रामाण्यादिभिर्ज्ञाप्यन्ते। तत्र निरूपणे सप्तम्यर्थो विषयत्वं, तस्य च हेत्वाभासत्वमित्यग्रेतनेनान्वयः।।

(सामान्यलक्षणम्)

2. **अनुमितीति।** अनुमितेः कारणीभूतो योऽभाव[9] स्तत्प्रतियोगि यद् यथार्थज्ञानं तद्विषयत्वमित्यर्थः। अस्ति च व्यभिचारादिग्रहसत्त्वेऽनुमितिप्रतिबन्धात् तदभावस्यानु[10] मितिहेतुतयाऽनु[11] मितिकारणीभूताभावप्रतियोगित्वं व्यभिचारादाविति। पर्वतो वह्न्यभाववान् इत्यादिभ्रमादप्यनुमिति प्रतिबन्धात् तदभावस्यानुमितिहेतुतया तत्प्रतियोगिज्ञानविषयत्वस्य वह्न्यभावादौ[12] सत्त्वात्रतातिव्याप्तिवारणाय **यथार्थपदम्**। तत्त्वञ्च भ्रमसामान्यभिन्नत्वम्[13] अतो वह्न्यभावस्य भ्रम[14] स्यांशिकप्रमात्वेऽपि न तद्दोषतादवस्थ्यम्। कामिन्यादावतिव्याप्तिवारणाय ज्ञानपदम्। न च व्यभिचारज्ञानाद्यभावस्य व्याप्त्यादिज्ञानेनान्यथासिद्धत्वात् तदभावस्यानुमित्यहेतुत्वात्[15] व्यभिचारादावव्याप्तिरिति वाच्यम्। आचार्यमतेनैतल्लक्षण-करणात्। तथाच तन्मते साध्यव्याप्यवान् पक्षः साध्यवान् इत्याकारिकैवानु[16] मितिरिति

नानुपपत्तिः। <u>केचित्तु</u> साध्यव्याप्यपक्षतावच्छेदकिकां साध्यव्याप्यविषयकसमूहालम्बनात्मिकां वा अनु[17] मितिमादाय मणिकृन्मतेनैव लक्षणं सङ्गमयन्ति। तदसत्। सर्वस्य सर्वत भ्रमानुमितौ मानाभावात् यत्र तादृशानुमितिः[18] कदापि नोत्पन्ना तत्रत्यदोषेऽव्याप्तिप्रसङ्गात्।[19] न च ह्रदो वह्निमान् घटत्वादित्यादौ वह्न्यभाववद्घटेऽतिव्याप्तिः। घटत्ववति वह्न्यभाववत्तानिश्चय[20] स्यापि वह्निव्याप्यघटत्ववद्ह्रदो वह्निमान् इत्याकारकानुमितिविरोधित्वादिति वाच्यम्। साध्याभाववतः साधनवतोऽपि <u>मणिकृन्मते</u> सव्यभिचारत्वेन तस्य लक्ष्यत्वात्।[21] न चैतस्य हेतुदोषलक्षणत्वेऽग्रेति चेत्यनेन दुष्टहेतुविभागानुपपत्तिरिति वाच्यम्। अनुमितिकारणीभूताभावप्रतियोगियथार्थज्ञानविषयो यत्रेति व्युत्पत्त्या दुष्टहेतुलक्षणमभिप्रेत्य तद्विभागः। ननु एतादृशज्ञानविषयत्वम् उदासीनघटादावतिव्याप्तं यद्विषयकत्वेन प्रतिबन्धकत्वम् इत्याद्युक्तावपि साध्यादावतिव्याप्तिः, न च यादृशविशिष्टविषयकत्वेन प्रतिबन्धकत्वं यथार्थज्ञानविषयीभूततादृशविशिष्टत्वं विवक्षितमिति वाच्यम्। यथार्थपदवैयर्थ्यापत्तेः, भ्रमस्थले विशिष्टस्याप्रसिद्धेः इत्यतो लक्षणान्तरमाह **यद्विषयकत्वेने**ति[22] <u>दीधितिकृतः</u>। <u>मिश्रास्तु</u>[23] प्रतिज्ञास्थहेत्वाभासपदं हेतोराभासा यत्र इति व्युत्पत्त्या दुष्टहेतुपरं, हेतोराभासा इति व्युत्पत्त्या च[24] हेतुदोषपरम्।[25] तत्र दुष्टहेतुलक्षणमाह–**अनुमितीति। अनुमितिकारणीभूताभावप्रतियोगिनो** ये तत्प्रकारकयथार्थज्ञानविषयत्वमित्यर्थः। इदञ्चज्ञायमानव्यभिचारादेः प्रतिबन्धकत्वमभ्युपेत्य। तथा च ज्ञायमानव्यभिचारादेरनुमितिप्रतिबन्धकतया साधनं साध्याभाववद्वृत्ति इत्याकारकं व्यभिचारादिप्रकारकं यद् यथार्थज्ञानं तद्विषयत्वं साधनेऽस्तीति लक्षणसङ्गतिः। वाच्यं प्रमेयं ज्ञेयत्वादित्यादिसद्धेतौ अनुमितिविरोधिनः साध्यासामानाधिकरण्यस्य भ्रमविषयतामादाय ज्ञेयत्वादिसद्धेतावतिव्याप्तिवारणाय[26] **यथार्थपदम्**। न चैवमपि निर्वह्निवृत्तित्वादेः कालिकादिसम्बन्धेन यथार्थज्ञानमादाय सद्धेतावति[27] व्याप्तितादवस्थ्यम्।[28] यादृशसम्बन्धेन ज्ञायमानस्य प्रतिबन्धकत्वं तादृशसम्बन्धेन तत्प्रकारकयथार्थज्ञानस्योक्तत्वात्। न च ह्रदो धूमत्ववान् धूमादित्यत्र बाधितहेतावव्याप्तिः, ह्रदनिष्ठधूमत्वाभावात्मकबाधस्य धूमहेतौ स्वरूपसम्बन्धेन यथार्थज्ञानासम्भवादिति वाच्यम्। तत्र साधननिष्ठव्यभिचारादेर्ज्ञानमादायैव[29] लक्षणसङ्गमनात् अग्रिमलक्षणद्वयञ्च हेतुदोषाणामिति वदन्ति। तदसत्। पर्वतो वह्निमान् धूमादित्यादौ धूमादिमद्धेतावतिव्याप्तेः।[30] पर्वतवृत्तितया ज्ञायमानस्य वह्न्यभावरूपबाधस्य स्वरूपसम्बन्धेन यद् यथार्थज्ञानं तद्विशेष्यत्वस्य धूमादौ सत्त्वात्। <u>गुरुचरणास्तु</u> प्रतिज्ञास्थहेत्वाभासपदं पूर्ववदुभयपरम्। तत्र दुष्टेहतुलक्षणमाह–**अनुमितीति।** स्वालङ्गकानुमिति[31] कारणीभूताभावप्रतियोगियथार्थज्ञानविषयत्वमित्यर्थः।[32] सर्वत्रैव दुष्टहेतोरन्ततो दुष्टज्ञान[33] विषयतामादायैव लक्षणसङ्गतिः। भगवज्ज्ञान-विषयतामादाय उदासीनघटादावतिव्याप्तिवारणाय **स्वलिङ्गकेति**। अनुमितिप्रतिबन्धकीभूतव्यभिचारभ्रमविषय[34] तामादाय सद्धेतावतिप्रसङ्गवारणार्थं भ्रमसामान्यभिन्नार्थक[35] यथार्थपदं सार्थकम्,

अग्रिमलक्षणद्वयञ्च हेतुदोषाणामिति प्राहुः। **यद्विषयत्वेनेति**। अत्र लिङ्गपदार्थोऽविवक्षितः। ज्ञानपदञ्च अप्रामाण्यज्ञानानास्कन्दितानाहार्यनिश्चयपरम्। तृतीयार्थोऽवच्छेदकत्वं, तच्चानतिरिक्तवृत्तित्वम्। तथाच यद्विषयकाप्रामाण्यज्ञानानास्कन्दितानाहार्यनिश्चयत्वम् अनुमितिप्रतिबन्धकतानतिरिक्तवृत्तित्वमित्यर्थः।[36] व्यभिचारादिनिश्चयसत्त्वेऽनुमित्यनुत्पादाद् व्यभिचारादिनिश्चयत्वं भवत्येवानुमितिप्रतिबन्धकतानतिरिक्तवृत्तीति व्यभिचारादौ लक्षणसङ्गतिः। न च साध्याभाववद्वृत्तित्वं व्यभिचारः, तन्निश्चयत्वञ्च नानुमितिप्रतिबन्धकतानतिरिक्तवृत्ति, निर्धर्मितावेच्छदकसाध्याभाववद्वृत्तित्वनिश्चयसत्त्वेऽप्यनुमित्युत्पादादिति[37] वाच्यम्। एतन्मते साध्याभाववद्वृत्ति[38] त्वविशिष्टसाधनतावच्छेदकावच्छिन्नस्यैव व्यभिचारत्वात्। न चैवं तद्वत्त्वं कथं हेतोरिति वाच्यं, कालिकादिसम्बन्धेन तस्यापि सम्भवात्। न च यद्विषयकत्वम् अनुमितिप्रतिबन्धकतानतिरिक्तवृत्ति तत्त्वमेवोच्यतामिति वाच्यम्। व्यभिचारादिविषयकत्वस्य अनुमित्यप्रतिबन्धकसंस्कारादावपि सत्त्वात् अनुमितिप्रतिबन्धकतातिरिक्तवृत्तित्वात् निश्चयत्वपर्यन्तम्। तादृशज्ञानत्वस्यानुमित्यप्रतिबन्धकबाधसंशयादावपि सत्त्वात् गुरोरपि निश्चयत्वस्य प्रवेशः।व्यभिचारादिविषयकनिश्चयत्वस्यानुमित्यप्रतिबन्धकाप्रामाण्यज्ञानानास्कन्दित[39] ज्ञानाहार्यज्ञानयोरपि[40] सत्त्वादनाहार्यान्तम्। अत्र च प्रमेयत्वविशिष्टव्यभिचारादावतिव्याप्तिवारणाय यद्विषयकतादृशनिश्चयत्वं,[41] यत्पक्षसाध्यहेतुकानुमितिप्रतिबन्धकतानतिरिक्तवृत्तिस्वानवच्छिन्नप्रकारतावच्छेदकतत्प्रतिबन्धकतानतिरिक्तवृत्तिविषयताकेनाघटितं तत्तत्पक्षहेतुसाध्यकानुमितौ[42] दोष इति विवक्षणीयम्। प्रमेयत्वविशिष्ट व्यभिचारादेश्च स्वानवच्छिन्नप्रकारतावच्छेदकशुद्धव्यभिवारादिघटितत्वान्नोक्तातिप्रसङ्गः। स्वानवच्छिन्नप्रकारतावच्छेदकतत्प्रति[43] बन्धकतानतिरिक्तिविषयताकघटितत्वञ्च प्रमेयत्वविशिष्टव्यभिचारादेरप्रसिद्धम्।[44] न चोक्तातिप्रसङ्गवारणाय स्वानवच्छिन्नप्रकारतावच्छेदकाघटितत्वेन यदर्थ एव विशिष्यतां[45] किमेतावता प्रयासेनेति वाच्यम्। प्रमेयत्वम् अवृत्ति प्रमेयत्वादित्यत्रवृत्तित्वाभाववद्वृत्तिप्रमेयत्वस्वरूपे व्यभिचारेऽव्याप्तेः। तस्य वृत्तिप्रमेयत्वात्मकबाधेन घटितत्वात्। उक्तविवक्षायाञ्च न दोषः, तादृशव्यभिचारज्ञानत्वावच्छिन्नं यत् प्रतिबन्धकत्वं तत्प्रतिबन्धकतानतिरिक्तवृत्तिविषयताकत्वाभावात् वृत्तिप्रमेयत्वात्मकबाधस्य बाधप्रतिबध्यतावच्छेदके[46] तल्लिङ्गकत्वादेरनिवेशात्। यन्मतेज्ञायमानव्यभिचारादिरेव प्रतिबन्धकस्तन्मते लक्षणमिदमसम्भवीति[47] लक्षणान्तरमाह—**ज्ञायमानमिति।** सिद्ध्यादावतिव्याप्तिवारणाय **ज्ञायमानमिति**। अत्रापि पूर्वोक्तदिशा निष्कर्षोऽवसेयः। ननु तत्पक्षहेतुसाध्यकानुमितिप्रतिबन्धकताघटितस्य लक्षणतया निर्वह्निः पर्वतो वह्निमान् इत्यादौ बाधादेर्हेत्वाभासत्वं न स्यात्। तत्पक्षसाध्य[48] कानुमितेर[49] प्रसिद्धेरिति चेन्न। यद्धर्मावच्छिन्नपक्षकयद्धर्मावच्छिन्नसाध्यकयद्धर्मावच्छिन्नहेतौ यावन्तो दोषाः सम्भवन्ति तावदन्यान्यत्वे तावन्मात्रविशेष्यकज्ञानविशेष्यत्वे वा तात्पर्यात्।

3. ननु दुष्टहेतोः पञ्चविधत्वम् असाधारणसत्प्रतिपक्षावादायैव, तच्च न सम्भवति। असाधारणतया नीयमाने शब्दपक्षकानित्यत्वसाध्यकशब्दत्वादिहेतौ सर्वसाध्यवत्साध्याभाववद्व्यावृत्तत्वरूपस्यासाधारण्यस्य सत्प्रतिपक्षताया[50] नीयमाने च शब्दो नित्यः शब्दत्वादित्यत्र शब्दो नित्यः[51] नित्यत्वव्याप्यासमवेत[52] द्रव्यत्वादौ साध्याभावव्याप्यवत्पक्षकत्वरूपस्य[53] सत्प्रतिपक्षत्वस्य च[54] विरहादित्यत आह—**दशाविशेष** इति। पक्षवृत्तिताभ्रमदशायां बाधनिश्चयविरहदशायाञ्च हेत्वोरेव, शब्दोऽनित्यः गगनात्, शब्दोऽनित्यः शब्दत्वात् इत्यत्रा[55] वृत्तिगगनादिशब्दत्वादिरूपदुष्टहेत्वोरेव। एवकारेण प्रागुक्तसद्धेतुपक्षावृत्तिहेत्वोर्व्यवच्छेदः। तथाच पक्षवृत्तिताभ्रमदशायाम् अवृत्तिगगनादेरसाधारणविधयानुमितिप्रतिबन्धकत्वात् शब्दोऽनित्यः कृतकत्वादित्यत्र शब्दनित्यत्वबाधनिश्चयविरहदशायाम् शब्दत्वहेतोः[56] सत्प्रतिपक्षविधयानुतितिप्रतिबन्धकत्वाच्च आभासत्वमित्यर्थः। केचित्तु[57] साध्य[58] व्यापकीभूताभावप्रतियागिहेतुमत्पक्षरूपस्य असाधारणत्वस्य साध्याभावव्याप्यवत्पक्षरूपस्य सत्प्रतिपक्षस्य च धियोऽनुमितिप्रतिबन्धके मानाभावः ग्राह्याभावानव[59] गाहितत्वादित्यत आह—**दशाविशेषे हेत्वो**रिति। एवकारो भिन्नक्रमे। असाधारणसत्प्रतिपक्षयोर्हेत्वोर्दशाविशेष एव सत्प्रतिपक्षासाधारणत्वेन[60] भानदशायामेवाभासत्वात्[61] अनुमित्यजनकत्वादित्यर्थः। एवकारेण तदज्ञानदशायान्तु जननादिति सूचितम्। तथाच अन्वयव्यतिरेकात्तज्ज्ञानस्य प्रतिबन्धकत्वमिति भावः।[62] तथाचैतदादायैव पञ्चविधत्वमुपपन्नमिति नव्याः। दीधितिकृतस्तु उक्तस्थलेऽव्याप्तिमाशङ्क्य तयोरलक्ष्यत्वेन तां निराकरोति **दशाविशेष** इति। हेतौ सर्वसाध्यवद्व्यावृत्तत्वस्य पक्षे साध्याभावव्याप्यस्य च भ्रमदशायामित्यर्थः। हेत्वोः सद्धेत्वोः। एवकारश्च प्रतिबन्धकत्वमित्यनन्तरं योज्यः। आभासत्वात् अनुमित्यजनकत्वात्।[63] तथा च दशाविशेषेऽनुमित्यजनकत्वात् अनुमितिप्रतिबन्धकत्वमेवेत्यर्थः। एवकारेण दोषत्वव्यवच्छेदः। अतएव दोषाणां नित्यत्वमेवेति प्राहुः। प्राञ्चस्तु सद्धेत्वो[64]रसाधारणसत्प्रतिपक्षयोरतिव्याप्तिमाशङ्क्य लक्ष्यत्वेन तां निराकुरुते दशाविशेष इति। तथा च यद्दशायां तद्बुद्धेरनुमितिप्रतिबन्धकत्वं तद्दशायां हेत्वाभासत्वमिष्टमेवेत्याहुः। तच्चिन्त्यम्।

4. नन्वेतावन्ति लक्षणानि बाधसत्प्रतिपक्षयोरतिव्याप्तानि, अनुमित्यसाधारणदोषस्यैवात्र लक्ष्यत्वात्तयोश्च प्रत्यक्षशाब्दज्ञानयोरपि प्रतिबन्धकतया केषाञ्चिद्दूषणमपाकरोति **यद्यपीति।**[65] वाधसत्प्रतिपक्षयोस्तदभावनिश्चयतदभावव्याप्यवत्तानिश्चययोः। **प्रत्यक्षशाब्देति।** सति घटाभावनिश्चयादौ घटवत्ता[66] प्रत्यक्षादेरनुदयादिति भावः। न च योग्यताज्ञानेनान्यथासिद्धतया बाधनिश्चयाभावादेर्न शाब्दहेतुत्वमिति कथमेतदिति वाच्यम्। योग्तताज्ञानोत्तरं लौकिकबाधनिश्चयादौ सति शाब्दानुदयात्[67] तदभावस्यापि शाब्द- हेतुत्वादित्याशयात्। न चोपमितिस्मृती किमिति नोट्टङ्किते इति वाच्यम्। उपमितेरतिरिक्त[68] प्रमात्वे विप्रतिपत्तेर्बा[69]धनिश्चयादिदशायां विशिष्टस्मरणानुत्पादस्य[70]

च उद्वोधकविरहेणापि सम्भवात् तत्र बाधनिश्चयाद्यभावस्य[71] हेतुत्वे मानाभावादित्याशयः।[72] वस्तुतः प्रत्यक्षेत्याद्युपलक्षणम्[73] तेऽपि द्रष्टव्ये। न लिङ्गाभासत्वमिति। अनुमित्यसाधारण- दोष एव हि हेत्वाभासः। अनुमित्यसाधारणत्वञ्च अनुमितितदितर-साधारणधर्मानवच्छिन्नानुमितिनिष्ठकार्यतानिरूपित[74] कारणतावत्त्वम्।[75] तच्च बाध निश्चयाभावादौ[76] नास्ति। तस्यानुमितित[77]दितरसाधारणजन्यत्वमिति व्युत्पत्त्या तद्विशिष्टबुद्धित्वस्येव कार्य्यता[78] वच्छेदकत्वादितिभावः। न च व्यभिचारादिज्ञानस्यापि व्याप्त्यादिप्रत्यक्षविरोधित्वात् बाधसत्प्रतिपक्ष-(AS2, बाधप्रतिपक्ष°)मात्रमधिकृत्य कथं शङ्केति वाच्यम्। तल्लिङ्गकतत्साध्यकानुमितित्वावच्छिन्नं प्रति तादृशव्यभिचार-ज्ञानत्वादिना स्वतः (AS2, कुतः) प्रतिबन्धकत्वमादृत्य तदघटितलक्षणाभिप्रायेणास्योक्त-त्वात्। **ज्ञायमानेति।** ज्ञायमान- दोषमात्रस्येत्यर्थः। ज्ञायमानदोषत्वञ्च साधारणदोषत्वेऽप्यक्षतमिति भावः। अभ्युपेत्यासाधारण्यमभ्युपपादयति।

5. ननु अनुमाननिरूपणप्रस्तावे प्रमाणसामान्यदोषाभिधानमनुचितमित्यनुशयेनाह- **यद्वेति। प्रत्यक्षादौ।** प्रत्यक्षसामग्र्यां सत्यां बाधेन बाधनिश्चयेन। इदमुपलक्षणं, तदभावव्याप्यवत्त्वादिनिश्चयेनेत्यपि द्रष्टव्यम्। ज्ञानं प्रत्यक्षाद्यात्मकं न प्रतिबध्यत इति। बाधनिश्चयसत्त्वेऽपि दोषविशेषादिजन्यज्ञानोदयादिति भावः। ननु बाधनिश्चय-सत्त्वेऽपि तद्विशिष्टप्रत्यक्षोत्पादे ततः प्रवृत्तिः स्यात् इत्यत आह-**किन्त्विति।** तत्र दोषविशेषजन्यज्ञाने (omitted in AS1), तथाचाप्रामाण्यज्ञानानास्कन्दित-(AS1, ०ग्रहानास्कन्दित०) ज्ञानस्यैव प्रवृत्तिहेतुतया नोक्तातिप्रसङ्ग इति भावः। अनुमितिस्तु बाधसत्त्वे (AS2, बाधनिश्चयसत्त्वे) न जायत एव इत्याह-**अनुमितौ त्वि**ति। तुकारेण प्रत्यक्षव्यवच्छेदः। **उत्पत्तिरेवेति। प्रतिवध्यत** इति। प्रागुक्तेनान्वयः। इदमापाततः। एतावतापि नासाधारण्यं दोषविशेषाद्यजन्यतद्विशिष्टबुद्धित्वस्यैव प्रतिबध्यतावच्छेदकत्वादिति दीधितिकृतः। नव्यास्तु (AS2, वयन्तु) प्रत्यक्षादाविति अस्यार्थः पूर्ववत् ज्ञानं ज्ञानत्वावच्छिन्नं, बाधनिश्चयादेर्न विशिष्टवुद्धित्वं प्रतिबध्यतावच्छेदकमिति फलितार्थः। उक्तयुक्तेरिति भावः। नन्वेवमुपनीतभानमपि बाधप्रतिबध्यं न स्यादित्यत आह-**किन्त्विति**। प्रतिस्विकरूपेणेति शेषः। तथाचानुमितितदितरसाधारणरूपेण कार्यतायाः (AS2, प्रतिबध्यताया) अभावात् असाधारणदोषत्वं बाधादेरिति भावः। शङ्कते **उत्पन्न इति**। तत्र दोषविशेषजन्यज्ञाने अप्रामाण्यम्, अप्रमात्वं दोषविशेषः। ज्ञाप्यते अनुमाना[79] नादिनेत्ति शेषः। तथा च प्रतिस्विकरूपेण प्रतिबध्यप्रतिबन्धक[80] भावकल्पने गौरवात् लाघवात्[81] दोषविशेषाद्यजन्यविशिष्टबुद्धित्वमेव बाधनिश्चयादिप्रतिबध्यतावच्छेदकमिति[82] नासाधारण्यमिति भावः। परिहरति-**अनुमितौ त्विति**। अनुशब्दः पश्चादर्थकः। पश्चात्त्वञ्च सौत्रोद्देशक्रमेण।[83] मितिः प्रमितिः। तुकारेण प्रत्यक्षमिति व्यवच्छेदः। तथाचानुमित्यादिप्रमितिषु उत्पत्तिरेवानित्यत्वमेव, न तु नित्यत्वं, प्रत्यक्षे तु[84]

नित्यत्वमनित्यत्वञ्चेत्यर्थ:। तथाच दोषविशेषाद्यजन्यविशिष्टबुद्धित्वस्य नित्यानित्य-वृत्तितया बाधनिश्चयाभावादे: कार्यतानवच्छेदकत्वमिति विशिष्टचाक्षुषत्वादेरेव[85] तथात्वं वाच्यमित्यसाधारणदोषत्वं बाधादेरक्षतमेव[86]। जन्यत्वस्य[87] कार्यतावच्छेदककोटौ निवेशे कालिकादिसम्बन्धेन[88] घटत्ववत्त्वादिकमादाय विनिगमनाविरहेण वहुतरगुरु-म्तरकार्यकारणभावकल्पनापत्तेरिति[89] दिगिति व्याचक्रु:।[90]

अत्रासिद्ध एव एको हेत्वाभास इति वास्तु।[91] असिद्धविरुद्धानैकान्तिकास्त्रय इति वल्लभाचार्या:।[92] उपाधिरसमर्थविशेषण[93] सिद्धसाधनञ्च एतत्त्रय[94] हेत्वाभास इति जरन्त:[95]। तदेतत् सकलं निराचिकीर्षु: दुष्टहेतून् विभजते[96] ते चेति। तत्पदं हेतुदोषपरं न तु दुष्टहेतुपरं, तेषामानन्त्यादसङ्गते:। चकारो यत इत्यर्थे। सव्यभिचारेत्यादौ भावार्थो[97] विवक्षित:। तथा च हेतुदोषा यत: सव्यभिचारत्वाद्यात्मका अत: पञ्चेत्यर्थ:[98] पञ्चत्वम् अपेक्षावुद्धिविशेष:। तथाच[99] हेतुदोषा: पञ्च सव्यभिचारत्वाद्यन्यतमत्वादित्य-नुमानमिति[100] भाव:।

References

1. AS1, ॐ नम: शिवाय
   AS2, ॐ नम: सरस्वत्यै
2. In the copy the reading is वेणूरावम्। The correct version is noted in the marginallia. H.P. Śāstri takes it as वूणूरावम् in the Descriptive Catalogue, of Asiatic Society the Calcutta, vol. XI, p. 151.
3. This verse is omitted in AS2.
4. AS2, व्यवस्थित्याति
5. तथाच is omitted in AS1.
6. AS1, ०मिति ध्येयं
7. AS1, ०काद०
8. AS2, ०प्यत्र
9. AS2, ०दिज्ञान०
10. AS2, ०वस्य अनु०
11. AS2, ०तया अनु०
12. AS2, ०भावे
13. AS1, ०भिन्नार्थकं
14. AS2, [illegible]
15. AS2, ०हेतुतया
16. AS1, ०कारिकुवा०
17. AS2, ०त्मिकाथाऽनु०
18. AS2, F 14a contains the following footnote-अत्र-साध्यव्याप्यवत्पर्वतो

वह्निव्याप्यधूमवान् इति परामर्शात् आचार्यमताभेद:

19. AS1, प्रसङ्गा:
20. AS1, ०वह्न्यभावनिश्चय०
21. AS2, लक्षणत्वात्
22. AS1, ०त्वेनेतीति०
23. AS1, मिश्रास्तु। मिश्रास्तु
24. च is omitted in AS2
25. AS1, ०परं च
26. AS2, ०सद्धेतौ अति०
27. AS2, ०ज्ञानमादायाति०
28. AS1, ०व्याप्तितादवस्थ्यात्
29. AS1, ०व्यभिचारदे . . .मादायव
30. AS2, ०वतिव्याप्ति:
31. AS1, स्वलिङ्गानुमिति०
32. AS1, ०विषयत्वमर्थ:
33. AS1, नित्यज्ञान०
34. AS1, ०व्यभिचारादिविषय०
35. AS2, ०भिन्नार्थं
36. AS1, ०वृत्तितद्वत्त्वमि०
37. AS2, ०नमित्युत्पदा०
38. AS1, ०साद्याभावद्वृत्ति०
39. AS2, ०ज्ञानास्कन्ति०
40. AS1, ०आहार्य्यज्ञानयोरपि०
41. AS1, यद्विषयकनिश्चयत्वं
42. AS1, तत्पक्षसाध्यकहेतुकानु०
43. AS1, ०च्छेदकत्वप्रति०
44. AS1, ०चारादारेवप्रसिद्धं०
45. AS1, विशिष्यन्तां
46. AS1, ०वध्यभावच्छे०
47. AS1, ०दमसमस्तवीति०
48. AS2, तत्पक्षकसाध्य०
49. AS1, ०कानुमितिर०
50. AS1, सपक्षतया
51. शब्दो नित्य: is omitted in AS1
52. AS1, ०व्यापकासम०
53. AS2, ०पक्षत्वरूपस्य०
54. सत्प्रतिपक्षत्वस्य च is ommitted in AS1
55. शब्दोऽनित्य: गगनात् . . . इत्यत्र is omitted in AS1

56. तथाच पक्षवृत्तिताभ्रमदशायाम् . . . . शब्दत्वहेतो: is omitted in AS1
57. This view is similar to that of Mathurānāth Tarkavāgḥīśa.
58. A similar text ननुसाध्य० etc. is found in the commentary of Rahasya by Mathurānātha Tarkavāgīśa, ed by. pt. Kāmākhyānatha Tarkavāgīśa 1990, vol. II, Part I, p. 778.
59. ०भावाद्यनव० ibid.
60. AS1, ०साधारणत्वे
61. AS1, भावदशा०
62. साध्यव्यापकी . . . प्रतिवन्धकत्वमिति भाव:–This portion is akin to the Commentary of *Rahasya* by Mathuranatha Tarkavagisha on *Tattracinatāmaṇi* of Gaṅgeśa.

—*The Tattvacintāmani,* ed. by K.N. Tarkavagisha, vol. II, part I, p. 778, 1990.

63. अनुमित्यजनकत्वात् is omitted in AS 2
64. AS1, सद्धेतो०
65. नन्वेतावन्ति . . . यद्यपीति–is omitted in AS2
66. AS2, घटवत्वा०
67. AS1, शब्दानु०
68. AS1, उपमानस्यातिरिक्त०
69. AS2, विप्रतिपत्ति०
70. AS1, ०स्मरणानुपादस्य
71. AS2, ०द्यभाव हेतुत्त्वे.
72. AS1, ०त्याशयवत्०
73. AS1, प्रत्यक्षानुमित्याद्यु०
74. AS2, प्रतिबध्यतानिरूपित०
75. AS2, प्रतिबन्धकताभावत्वं
76. AS2, ०निश्चयादौ
77. AS2, तस्य चानुमिति
78. AS2, प्रतिबध्यता०।
79. AS1, अनुमादिनेति
80. AS1, प्रतिप्रतिबन्धक०
81. लाघवात् is omitted in AS 1.
82. AS1, ०निश्चयप्रति०
83. AS1, , सौत्रोद्देस्य०
84. AS2, च
85. AS1, विशेष्य०
86. AS1, ०क्षमेव
87. AS2, जन्यतावच्छेदकस्य
88. AS2, कालिकसम्ब०

89. AS2, वहूतरकार्य०
90. AS2, व्रूम:
91. Footnote in Folia 147a/AS2 —(वाह्या: केचन जना:)
92. AS1, वल्लभाचार्य्य:
93. AS1, उपाधि०
94. एतत्त्रयं is omitted in AS 1
95. AS1, ज्वरन्त
96. AS2, विभजति
97. AS2, साधारणेति भावार्थो विवक्षित:
98. This portion is omitted in AS2
99. तथाच is omitted in AS1.
100. AS1, सव्यभिचारतत्वादितयनुमानमिति.

Index of References

(*Sāmānyanirukti*)

Sāmānyanirukti

English Translation

General Definition of *Hetvābhāsa*

1. The pseudo-reasons are taken for explanation because of the fact that determination of their essential character is the casual factor of achieving success (in a battle of debate).

2. Here the character of pseudo-reasons may mean objectivity to valid knowledge of the counter-positive relating to absence which stands as cause of inferential cognition, or that may mean the nature of impediment to inference caused by a particular object possessed by the cognition of the reason, or that may mean the essence of that which when presently known causes obstruction to the emergence of valid inference.

3. Because, in particular situations the so called reasons known as *Asādhārana* (the uncommon) and *Satpratipakṣa* (counter-balance) become pseudo-reasons and knowledge of them also causes obstruction to the origination of inferences.

4. Though *Bādha* (contradiction) and *Satpratipakṣa* (counter-balance) cause obstruction only to perception and verbal cognition and as such does not deserve the mark of pseudo reasons, still, this definition here is meant for the case of presently known faults of reason.

5. Or, the case may be that in perception etc. knowledge is not obstructed but invalidity is indicated to the knowledge produced out of them. In the case of inference the very emergence of it is obstructed. These faults are five in number i.e. *savyabhicāra, viruddha, satpratipakṣita, asiddha* and *bādhita,* (violation, opposition, counterbalanced, unfounded and contradiction).

Here ends the explanation of the general definition of pseudo-reason under the topic on pseudo-reason in the Second Book known as Anumāna in the Tattvacintāmaṇi composed by Śri Gaṅgeśopādhyāya.

Kaṇādaṭippanī

English Translation

(Commentary of *Kaṇāda Tarkavāgīśa*)

1. (Benedictory Verse) After meditating on the deity (i.e. Krisña) who possesses the pollens of budding lotus presented to the feet having the colour of Durvā-grass the author Kaṇāda by name discloses at large the thoughtprovoking indepth meaning of the text of *Cintāmaṇi.*

Atha etc. This conveys the sense that after interpreting the reason along with pervasion and allied concepts. *Hetvābhāsa* means defects of the reason. *Tattvanirṇaya* etc. Here it is indicated that interpretation of the essence of the means of knowledge and achievement of victory by the contender are the causal factors. The import of the sentence is that by pursuing such method the establishment of valid nature of the reason embraced by the contender and the faulty character of the reason embraced by the opponent happens and that leads to the occurence of determination of the real essence. The relevance of interpretaion of pseudo-reason takes place for its serving the same purpose,—it indicates. It is not that interpretation of smoke etc. also becomes relevant. Because, though that plays a causal factor to the victory of the proponent in the matter of acquiring real essence of things that serves no utility. It cannot be put to quesion that why dogmas of both less and excessive coverage are left out of consideration on the ground that they are helpful to the determination of real essence of objects. Because, a pseudo-reason which aises in mind in the relation of opposition etc. by the reason due to self-dominated conduct of volition etc. deserves not to be ignored. In this connection contextual relevance also should be taken into consideration. The word *nirupyante.* This means—made known by the charater of definition and evidential means. In the word *nirupane* the seventh case-ending denotes objectivity and that is related to the character of pseudo-reason mentioned afterwards

General Definition of Pseudo-Reason (*Hetwābhāsa*)

2. The indicative word *anumiti.* This conveys the sense of that objectivity in connection with that valid cognition of counter-corralate of that absence which stands as causal factor to inference.

The character of countercorrelate of absence standing as causal factor to inference exsits in violation (*vyabhicāra*) etc. This is established from the fact that emergence of inference becomes obstructed in the presence of cognition of violation etc. This in turn proves that absence of that (violation) is the cause of inferential cognition. As the erroneous cognition like 'the mountain is possessed of absence of fire' makes opposition to the emergence of inferential cognition absence of such erroneous cognition is liable to be admitted as causal factor of inference. In such a case the objectivity to cognition of counter-correlate of that absence happens to exist in the absence of fire and the like. In order to avoid over-applicability to such case the word *yathārtha* (meaning valid) is inserted here. The word *tattva* means the nature of what is other than error in general. As a result, though the error in the form of absence of fire contains validity to some extent the situation of containing that fault does not occur. The word *Jñāna* (i.e. cognition) is incorporated to avoid overextension to damsel (*kāminī*) and the like. It cannot be argued that absence of knowledge of violation falls under conditionality (out of the purview of cause) by the cognition of pervasion etc and in consequence the absence of that does not become the causal factor of inference resulting in under-coverage to violation and the like. Because, the definition here is formulated following the opinion of *Ācārya* (i.e. *Udayanācārya*). According to him (Acārya) the inference takes place in the following form—the subject pervaded by the probandum possesses the probandum. Therfore, no question of incompetency arises. However, there are others who attempt to explain relevance of the definition in the line of the author of *Cintāmaṇi* himself taking a piece of inference that incorporates totality of objects pervaded by the probandum or that delimits the subject-essence pervaded by the probandum. That is not justified. Everything is not valid in all cases of erroneous inference. Therefore the fault of narrowness occurs in the cases of those faults where such erroneous inference is not generated at all. It cannot be argued that the definition becomes overextended to the case of inference like 'the lake contains fire due to the existence of potness' on the ground that even the knowledge of certainty in respect of possessing the absence of fire in the location of what possesses potness poses opposition to the emergence of inference in the form—'the lake characterised by potness pervaded by fire contains fire.' Even the case of possessor of the probans in relation to the absence of probandum contains the fault of violation and that is an object of the definition according to the author of the *Maṇi*-text. Nor can it be argued that as it is the defintion of the faults of probans the division of feigned reason by the text *agre ca* (अंग्रे च) goes irrelevant. The division of feigned reason has been made in consideration of its defintion in the sense arising out of the following derivation—where there exists the object of valid knowledge—the object which has become the counter-positive of absence that attends to causality of inferential cognition. Now an objection may be raised. For instance, objectivity to such type of cognition is overapplicable to non-contextual pot and the like. In spite of utterance of the clause 'the impediment caused by the object involving it' over-applicability occurs to probandum and the like. This cannot be supported by saying that the same sort of qualifiedness in respect of object of valid knowledge which plays the role of causal factor to the impediment is the intended meaning in the present case. In that case the insertion of the word *yathārtha* (valid) will be futile. Moreover, in the erroneous inference the qualified is not existent at all. For this reason the author speaks another definition with words *yadviṣayakatvena* etc. formulated by the author of *Dīdhiti.* Miśra however explains the word *Hetvābhasa* attached to *Pratijñā* in the following way. From the derivation as residence of faults of the reason the word means pseudo-reason and from the other derivation as fualts of the reason it denotes faults residing in the reason. Now the definition of pseudo-reason is told by the sentence of *Anumiti* etc. That is indicative of the objectivity in relation to valid knowledge caused by such characters which become counter-correlate of absence becoming the causal factor of inferential cognition. This happens by taking cognizance of the character of making obstruction belonging to violation etc. congized presently. Now as violation etc. known presently possesses the character of making obstruction to inference the objectivity to that valid knowledge which is caused by the character of violation etc. in the form 'the probans resides in a location which contains absence of the probadum,' verily exists in the probans and thus occurs releavance to the definition. The word *yathārtha* (i.e. valid) is included in the definition in order to overcome the situaion of over-applicabiliy to valid probans like the property of knowable etc. taking non-coexistence of the probandum happened to be contradictory to inference as objectivity to errors in the matter of valid reason like 'what is expressible is object of means of knowledge because of its possessing the attribute of knowability.' It cannot be argued that in spite of that attempt over-applicability to valid reason will occur as usual taking knowledge of presence in a fireless location as valid in the relation like temporal etc. The knowledge of valid knowledge has been spoken of as caused by that character and that relation by which what is presently known plays the role of an obstructor. It will not be proper to say that the fault of underextension will occur to contradicted reason in the case of inference like 'the lake possesses the attribute of smoke because it contains smoke' on the force of the argument that the knowledge of contradiction in the form 'absence of the attribute of smoke in the location of lake' is impossible to be valid in smoke, the reason in the relation of self-nature. The definition will suit to that case only on acceptance of cognition of violation and the like present in the reason. The two definitions that come forward actually relate to faults of the reason, they say. This, however, is not acceptable. Because there occurs over-applicability to the valid reason in the case of inference like 'the mountain possesses fire due to existence of smoke in it.' It so happens because there exists in smoke in the relation of self-same the subjectessence of that valid cognition which pertains to contradiction in the form of absence of fire known as presently existing in the mountain. According to our preceptor the word *Hetvābhāsa* in the sentence of Declaration denotes both of them like the previous case. The author speaks of the definition of feigned reason by the sentence *Anumiti* etc. This conveys the sense of contentness relating to valid knowledge of countercorrelate of the absence which is supposed to be the causal factor of inference caused by its own reason. In each case conformity to the definition will occur at least with the acceptance of the object-essence of invalid cognition realating to the feigned reason. The word *Svaliṅgaka* is inserted to counteract the occurence of over-appilcability to non-contextual pot etc. with the acceptance of object-essence of knowledge of God. The word *Yathārtha* conveying the sense of opposed to error in general becomes meaningful only for counteracting the occurence of over-application to valid reason happened with the acceptance of objectness relating to erroneous cognition of violation which becomes the causal factor of making obstacale to the emergence of inference. The two definitions that come next relate to feigned reason, the author says. The sentence starting with *Yadviṣayatvena* etc. Here the meaning of the word reason is not intended. The word *Jñāna* is denotative of certainty which is unimposed and not traversed by knowledge of invalidity. The third case-ending here means delimitorness and that again is indicative of presence in location not going above the limit of extension. In this process this leads to convey certitude unaffected by imposition and inclusion into knowledge of invalidity of whatsoever object. To be more clear this means presence in a location not going above the limit of extension relating to the nature of impediment to inferential cognition. In the presence of confirmation of violation inferential cognition does not emerge, This surely proves that confirmation of violation etc. is not extended above the limit of the attribute of impediment to inference and hence the definition will conform to violation etc. It cannot he argued that violation means presence in the location of absence of the inferable property and its certainty does not occur to a location not over-exetensive to the limit of obstacleness to inference, because inference does not generate in the availability of certainty of existence in a location of the absence of the inferable property which is the de-limitor of the nature of attributeless. According to this view the property of violation goes to what is delimited by the delimitor of the property of the reason qualified by the property of existence in the location of the absence of the inferable property. It cannot be questioned why the nature of becoming that sort goes to the reason, because that may be achieved to that in temporal relation also. It should not be argued that let the essence of that alone—the objectivity of what is not present beyond the limit of attribute of obstacle to inferential cognition be uttered. Because, the causality of object like violation and the like exist even in impression and the like which are not supposed to be obstacle to inferential cognition and they are present to such location which cross the limit of the attribute of obstacle to inferencial cognition. That is why the definition is extended upto the word *niscayatva* (i.e. certainty). As the attribnte of such cognition belongs even to doubt of contradiction etc. which are not abstructor of inference the property of certainty though heavy has been inserted. The definition has been prolonged upto *anāhārya* (not to be imposed) owing to the reason that knowledge of imposition and knowledge which is not traversed by the cognition of invalidity which does not cause obstruction to the inference of certainty caused by the object of violation and the like lay their presence. Here, in order to avoid over-application to violation etc. qualified by the attribute of the knowable the word signifying such knowledge of certainty containing a specific object is introduced. The fault should be understood in the inference caused by that subject, reason and inferable property where such knowledge of certainty caused by a certain object is not happened by the causality of objectessence present not beyond the limit of the attribute of obstructor which becomes the delimitor of characteressence not delimited by itself and not present outside the purview of obstructorness of inference accomodating the specific subject, inferable property and reason. And this type of over-application mentioned here does not occur to violation and the like qualified by the attribute of knowables, because they are caused by pure violation which is the delimitor of character-essnece not delimited by the self. The attribute of being caused by the causality of objectivity residing in what is not other than the attribute of that obstructor which is the delimitor of character-essence not delimited by the self is not familiar in connection with the violation qualified by the attribute of knowables. It can not be argued that in order to check the over-applicability mentioned above let that be qualified by whatsover meaning, because that is not caused by the delimitor of character—essence delimited not by the self, what is the use of making these efforts? Because, under-applicability occurs to violation in the form of knowableness which resides in the location of non-existence of absence in the case of inference like 'knowableness contains absence due to its containing the attribute of knowables.' This happens because of the fact that it is caused by obstruction of the nature of knowables in the form of presence. There will be no harm if the aforesaid meaning is taken as intended (by the author). Because, there is absence of being generated by the content-essence lying in a location not different from the attribute of the obstructor which is delimited by the attribute of cognition of such violation and the other thing is that there is no inclusion of the causality of that reason in the delimiting attribute of being obstructed by contradiction in the form of present knowableness. In spite of that the definition suffers from impossibility in the opinion of those who recognise violation becoming an object of present cognition as real obstructor. That is why the author mentions another definition such as Jñāyamānam etc. The word *jñāyamānam* is inserted in order to debar over-applicability to what is establishment and the like. Here also the purport should be extracted in the aforesaid way. Now an objection may be raised in the following way. As the definition relates to what is caused by obstructorness in connection with inference generated by that subject, reason and the inferable property contradiction and the like in the inference like 'fireless mountain possesses fire,' fails to deserve the attribute of feigned reason. If it is argued that such type of inference which is caused out of that subject and inferable property is not established that will not be justified. Because, the implied meaning refers either to subjecthood of cognition caused by that much of the subject or to eitherness of the given alternatives of the number of faults that occur in the reason delimited by the specific attribute caused by inferable property limited by a specific attribute as well as by the subject limited by a specific attribute.

3. Another argument may be advanced here. The fivefold division of feigned reason occurs with the very inclusion of the uncommon and the counter-balanced. That fails to become possible. If we take the illustration of inference constituted by sound as subject, transitoriness as inferable property and the property of sound as reason as a case of uncommon (*asādhāraṇa*) we shall be failing due to non-existence of the fault of uncommon in the form of difference from the location of all inferable and non-inferable properties. Similarly, we shall be failing if we take the inference like 'sound contains eternity as there is the property of sound in it' as a case of counterbalanced on the ground of absence of the property of counter-balanced in the form of subjecthood present in a location pervaded by the absence of the inferable property in the counter-inference like 'sound possesses the property of enternity due to its containing the property of substance which is not inherent in what is pervaded by eternity.' That is why the author opens the clause *daśāviśesa* etc. In the case of erroneous cognition of presence in the subject and in the case of absence of confirmation of contradiction the effect goes to the two reasons. In the instance of inference like 'sound is noneternal, because that contains sky' and in another instance like 'sound is non-eternal because that possesses the property of sound' the effect goes to two feigned reasons like 'absent sky' etc. and 'the property of sound' etc. The word *eva* is introduced to differentiate the two reasons mentioned above which are not present in the subject of valid inference. In this way, in the situation of erroneous cognition of presence in the subject 'absent sky' etc. causes obstruction to inference and therefore becomes faulty reason in the capacity of what is known as uncommon. In the same way following the inference like 'sound is non-eternal, because it possesses the attribute of the generated' while there arises the situation of negation of confirmation of contradiction in connection with the eternality of sound the reason like attribute of sound becomes feigned reason due to its causality to obstruct inference in the capacity of what is known as counter-balanced. Some logicians, however, deny the reasonableness of obstruction to cognition in connection with the fault of the uncommon in the form of a subject possessed of the reason as counterpositive of negation which is supposed to be the pervader of the inferable property as well as in connection with the fault of the counterbalanced in the form of a

subject possessed of what is pervaded by the negation of the inferable property. The argument is that they do not contain involvement of the absence of acceptability. That is why the author takes resort to the clause *daśāviśeṣe hetvoriti.* The word *eva* is used to denote different order. Only in a particular situation in connection with the two faulty reasons, the uncommon and the counterbalanced, i.e. while they appear in cognition as counterbalanced and uncommon they are recognised as faulty reasons, so to say they fail to generate valid inference. The word *eva* denotes that while they are not known as such they generate (inference). Now, the implication is that by the process of agreement by presence and disagreement by absence the attribute of the obstructor goes to knowledge of them. Following this principle alone the neo-ligicians establish reasonableness of the five-fold division. The author of *Dīdhiti,* however, explains the term *daśāviseṣa* in the following sense:—anticipating the fault of narrowness in the above-mentioned illustration they become out of purview of the definition and in order to cure that fault the author resorts to the clause *daśāviśeṣa* etc. This means, in the situation of error of the attribute of what is differentiated from all locations of the inferable property in the reason and of what is pervaded by the absence of the inferable property in the location of the subject. *Hetvoh* means relating to twin reasons which are valid. The word *eva* should be added after the word *pratibandhakatvaṁ. Ābhāsatvāt* means not being the generator of infernatial cognition. In this way, not being the generator of inference in particular situations means the attribute of obstructor to inference. The word *eva* differentiates faultness. For these reasons, they argue that these faults are verily eternal. The ancient logicians however explain that the word *daśāviśeṣa* has been employed to cure the over-applicability of the fault of uncommon and counterbalanced to valid reasons coming under the purview of the definition. Thus they argue that their conṭaining the character of feigned reason is desirable in that situation in which the cognition of them causes obstruction to inference. But their argument awaits criticism.

4. Now, one may argue that these definitions are liable to be over-applicable to contradiction and counterbalaced. Because, the specific fault relating to inference alone is definable here. But those two faults cause obstruction even to perception and verbal cognition. In order to overcome these objections levelled by some the author mentions *yadyapi* etc. Relating to contradiction and counterbalanced means relating to confirmation of its absence and to confirmation of being possessed of the pervasion of its absence. *Pratyakṣaśābda*

relating to absence of a pot the perception of the character of what possesses a pot does not emerge. One cannot question why this happens on the plea that the absence of confirmation of contradiction and the like are made superfluons by the knowledge of fitness and therfore they are not causal factors of verbal cognition. Because, even after knowledge of fitness verbal cognition does not arise in case there happens confirmation of normal contradiction and the like and therfore, absence of them (i.e. confirmation of contradiction etc.) also happens to be recognised as generating factor of verbal cognition. Nor can it be questioned why comparison and recollection are not mentioned in this case. Because, whether knowledge emerging out of comparison is a different sort of valid knowledge or not is a matter of controversy, and non-emergence of specific recognition in the situation of confirmation of contradiction etc. becomes possible due to absence of indicator also. The intention, therefere, is that there is no ground for accepting the causality of absence of confirmation of contradiction etc. In fact, the word pratyakṣa (perception) etc. is indicative of the sense that those two also should be taken into consideration. The word *liṅgābhāsatvam* etc. *Hetvābhāsa* or feigned reason stands for only the specific fault of inference. *Anumityasādhāraṇatva* or specific in connection with inference means the attribute of what possesses causality described by effectness belonging to inference delimited by the attribute common to inference and what is other than inference. That does not belong to absence of certitude of contradiction etc. That contains the character of produced from inference and what is other than inference in common.

If it is argued that knowledge of violation etc. also obstructs perception of pervasion etc., then why the apprehension is raised only in connection with contradiction and counterbalanced? This question is not reasonable. Because, that has been mentioned keeping the definition in veiw involving those things after accepting the intrinsic character of obstructor by the attribute of cognition of such violation towards what is delimited by the attribute of inference caused by that reason and that inferable property. *Jñāyamāna* etc. This relates only to faults which are objects of current knowledge. The attribute of presently known fault remains unimpaired in spite of its being a common fault. *Abhyapetya* means the uncommon character is being established.

5. Now the author thinks that in the topic of determining inference mentioning of faults relating to means of knowledge in general is unjust and that is why he writes *yad vā iti. Pratyakṣādau*

etc. In the situatioin where the constituent factors of perception remain present. *Bādhena* means by certain knowledge of contradiction. This is indicative. This includes the sense of the causality of confirming knowledge of the attribute of the location of what is pervaded even by its absence. *Jñānaṁ* refers to knowledge in the form of perception and the like. This is related to *pratibadhyate* etc. This means to say that in spite of the presence of certitude of contradiction cognition caused by specific faults takes place. It may be apprehended that if in the very presence of certitude of contradiction specific perception of that arises then let there be action also. In order to answer that apprehension the author writes *kintu* etc. *Tatra* refers to knowledge produced out of a kind of fault. The aforesaid over-application does not take place, because, only that sort of knowledge which is not grasped by knowledge of invalidity is the cause of action. Inference does not arise at all in existence of contradiction and that is why the author writes *anumitau tu iti.* The indeclinable *tu* is employed to discriminate perception. *Utpattireveti* etc. *Pratibadhyate* etc. That is related to what is mentioned earlier. This is for the time being. According to the author of *Dīdhiti* this much also is not sufficient for producing unique character. Because, the delimiting attribute of what is obstructed goes to the character of that qualified cognition which is not produced by any sort of faults. According to our opinion the meaning of the text *pratyakṣādi* etc. should run thus:—knowledge like previous cases is delimited by knowledge-essence. The attribute of qualified cognition in connection with confirmation of contradiction etc. is not the delimiting attribute of the state of being obstructed. This follows from the above-mentioned argument. It may be apprehended that in that case knowledge accrued from supra-normal sense-object relation also will fail to become obstructed by contradiction. That is why the author moves to write *kintu* etc. This relates to indicating their causality in individual form. In this way as there occurs absence of the state of being obstructed in common with inference and other than inference the fault of contradiction etc. will be transformed into the fault of the uncommon in consequence. The author denotes apperhension with the word *utpanna* etc. Invalidity of knowledge produced out of a particular fault is equivalent to the state of invalid knowledge . . ., it means. *Jñāpyate* means 'made known'and that happens through inference and the like. Now, the projection of the obstructor and the obstructed relation to each case taken individually will entail the fault of cumberness. It is for the sake of simplicity that we are to accept the state of qualified cognition not generated by any particular fault as the delimiting attribute of the state of the fault of uncommon. The author avoids the situation with sentence starting with *anumitau tu* etc. The word *anu* conveys the sense of afterwards. The sense of afterwards follows the order of enumeration of rules. *Miti* means knowledge. By the word *tu* the defferentiation of perception is made. In the varieties of cognition like inference etc. there is generation i.e. the state of non-eternal and not the state of eternality. In this way as the state of qualified cognition not generated by any specific fault resides in both eternal and not-eternal entities absence of confirmation of contradiction etc. fails to possess the delimiting attribute of productivity. That qualification should be spoken of in connection with the state of qualified visuality alone and thus the state of being the fault of uncommon will remain unimpaired in the ground of contradiction etc. It is explained that if the state of being generated is incorporated in the clause of the delimitor of productivity due to lack of any definite criteria the state of being the possessor of potness will be possible to cite in the relation of temporal and others and there will arise the apprehension of projecting multifarious complicated cause and effect relations.

Let there be only one type of feigned reason called *asiddha* (unfounded), say some logicians of other disciplines. Vallabhacharya speaks of three fallacies known as *asiddha* (unfounded), *viruddha* (opposed), and *anaikāntika* (partial violation). Some old logicians accept *upādhi,* (vitiating condition), *asamarthaviśeṣaṇam* (uncapable adjective), and *siddhasādhanam* (founding of the already founded) as fallacies. In order to counteract all such views the author divides feigned reasons with the sentence *te ceti.* The word *tat* stands for the fault of the reason, not for the faulting reason, because that will be out of relevance due to their innumerability. The word *ca* is used in the sense of the word *yataḥ* (because). The intended implication relates to the fault of violation etc. As the faults of reason are in the form of the attribute of violation and the like they are five in number, it means. The number five is a kind of *apekṣābuddhi* (knowledge dependant upon sense of relativity). In this way there will arise the inferential cognition like—'faults of the reason are five in number, because they belong to any of the attributes like the state of violation and the like'.

APPENDIX- I

रघुनाथशिरोमणेः

सामान्यनिरुक्तिदीधितिः

1. एतावता प्रबन्धेन सपरिकरं हेतुं निरूप्य तत्प्रसङ्गात् तत्त्वनिर्णयादिरूपतत्कार्य्य-कारित्वाच्च तदाभासनिरूपणं प्रतिजानीते अथेति।
2. अनुमितीति, यथाश्रुतमिदं हेतुदोषाणां लक्षणं तद्वत्वञ्च दुष्टहेतूनां तदभिप्रायेणैव उपधेयसङ्करेऽपीत्यादि वक्ष्यति। तत्रानुमितिपदम् अनुमितिनिष्ठकार्य्यतानिरूपक-सम्बन्धित्वेनानुमितितत्कारणज्ञानपरं साध्यव्याप्यहेतुमान् पक्षः साध्यवानित्या-कारानुमितिपरं वा, तेनैकत्र हेतौ व्यभिचारादिग्रहेऽप्यन्यस्य परामर्शादनुमित्युत्पादेन व्यभिचाराद्व्याप्त्यादिज्ञानेनान्यथासिद्धत्वाच्च व्यभिचारादिग्रहाभावस्यानुमित्यजन-कत्वेऽपि न क्षतिरिति वदन्ति। पर्वतो निर्वह्निर्धूमो वह्नेरभिधेयत्वं वा मेयत्वस्य व्यभिचारीत्यादिभ्रमादनुमितिप्रतिबन्धादाह यथार्थेति। ननु प्रतिबन्धकज्ञान-विषयव्यभिचारादिघटकसाध्यादेरपि प्रत्येकं हेत्वाभासतापत्तिः। अथ विशिष्टविषयज्ञानं प्रतिबन्धकं तद्घटकञ्च न विशिष्टमिति चेत्तर्हि यथार्थेति व्यर्थं भ्रमविषयविशिष्टस्याप्रसिद्धत्वादित्यनुशयेनाह यदिति। केचित्तु दुष्टानामेव हेतूनामेतानि लक्षणानि, तत्र तृतीयमिव प्रथममपि ज्ञायमानव्यभिचारादेः प्रतिबन्धकत्वमभ्युपेत्य तदर्थञ्च तादृशाभावप्रतियोगिनो ये व्यभिचाराद-यस्तत्प्रकारकयथार्थज्ञानविषयत्वमग्रे च तत्त्वमित्यस्य तद्वत्त्वमित्यर्थः आद्यस्यैव वा दुष्टहेतुलक्षणत्वमिति प्राहुः। लिङ्गमविवक्षितं यद्विषयत्वेन यादृशविशिष्टविषय-त्वेन, तेनानुमितिप्रतिबन्धकपक्षविशेष्यकभ्रमविषये साध्याभावादौ सद्धेत्वादिनिष्ठे नातिप्रसङ्गः, अवच्छेदकञ्चेहानतिरिक्तवृत्तित्वं, तेन विशिष्टस्यासत्वेऽपि भ्रमात् प्रतिबन्धेऽपि न क्षतिः विशेषणीयञ्च तादृशविशिष्टान्तराघटितत्वेन, तेन प्रमेयत्वादिविशिष्टे सव्यभिचारादौ नातिप्रसङ्गः, एवञ्च पक्षतावच्छेदकादिविरह-

विशिष्टः, पक्षः पक्षनिष्ठस्तद्विरहो वा साध्याभाववद्वृत्ति साधनं साधनवद्वृत्ति-साध्याभावो वा हेतुदोषः, येन केनापि सम्बन्धेन तद्वांश्च प्रकृतो हेतुर्दुष्टः यादृशधर्मिणि यादृशधर्म्मवत्ताज्ञानं अनुमितिप्रतिबन्धकं तस्य धर्म्मिणस्तादृश-धर्म्मवत्वं हेतुदोष इत्यपि कश्चित्। अथ पर्वतत्वेन पक्षत्वे वह्नित्वेन साध्यत्वे विशिष्टधूमत्वेन च हेतुत्वे पर्वतादेः काञ्चनमयत्वविरहो ह्रदस्य वह्निधूमशून्यत्वं पर्वतस्य महानसीयवह्निधूमविरहित्वं मेयत्वस्य केवलधूमस्य वा वह्निव्यभिचारो विशिष्टस्य धूमस्य वा पर्वतीयवह्निव्यभिचारो न दोषः न वा तत्सम्बन्धेन तत्र तस्य हेतोर्दुष्टत्वम् अतस्तद्धर्म्मावच्छिन्नतत्पक्षकतद्धर्म्मावच्छिन्नतत्साध्यकतद्धर्म्मा-वच्छिन्नतद्धेतुकानुमितिप्रतिबन्धकत्वं वाच्यं, तथाच निर्वह्निः पर्वतो वह्निमान् पर्वतावृत्तिवह्निमान् वा तद्व्यभिचारिणः पर्वतावृत्तेर्वा धर्म्मादित्यादौ न कोऽपि हेत्वाभासः स्यात् तादृशानुमितेरप्रसिद्धत्वादिति। अत्र वदन्ति यद्विषयनिश्चयस्य विरोधिविषयताप्रयुक्तस्तदुत्तरम् अनुमितौ अनाहार्य्यमानसज्ञाने वा पक्षतावच्छेदक-विशिष्टपक्षे साध्यतावच्छेदकविशिष्टसाध्यवैशिष्ट्यावगाहित्वस्य साध्यतावच्छेदक-विशिष्टसाध्यनिरूपितव्याप्तिविशिष्टहेतुतावच्छेदकविशिष्टहेतुमत्त्वावगाहित्वस्य च द्वयोर्व्यतिरेकस्तत्त्वं हेतुदोषत्वं पक्षतावच्छेदकवैशिष्ट्यादिकञ्च वैज्ञानिकं न तु वास्तवं ग्राह्यं व्यापिश्चान्वयतो व्यतिरेकतश्च वाच्या, तादृशावगाहित्वप्रसिद्धि-राहार्य्यज्ञान एवाभ्युपेतव्यानन्यगतिकत्वात्। एवञ्च वस्तुमात्रनिश्चयादनन्तरं निर्वह्नित्वाविशिष्टे वह्नेरग्रहेऽपि न क्षतिस्तस्य विरोध्यविषयकत्वात्। एवं साध्यनिश्चयोत्तरं तस्याननुमितावपि मानसज्ञानाविरोधित्वाच्च तादृशि पक्षे तादृशसाध्यवैष्ट्यिस्य तादृशसाध्यनिरूपितव्याप्तिविशिष्टतादृशहेतुवैशिष्ट्यस्य चावगाहिनो ज्ञानस्य यद्विषयं ज्ञानं विरोधिविषयकं तत्त्वं तादृशज्ञानविरोधित्वं वा हेतुदोषत्वं, ज्ञानविरोधित्वञ्च तद्विषयविषयकग्रहविरोधिग्रहविषयत्वम्। एवंविधैव रीतिरुत्तरत्र सर्वत्र सव्यभिचारलक्षणादावनुसर्त्तव्या इत्यपि केचित्। केचित्तु यादृशपक्षकयादृशसाध्यकयादृशहेतौ यावन्तो दोषाः सम्भवन्ति तावदन्यान्य-त्वमेकमात्रदोषस्थले च तत्त्वमेव हेत्वाभासत्वं स चातिरिक्त एवान्योऽन्याभाव इति न वैयर्थ्यं पञ्चविधभेदोक्तिस्तु तत्सम्भवस्थलाभिप्रायेण व्यभिचारादेः साध्यादिभेदनियन्त्रितत्वात् शब्दाभेदमात्रस्य चाकिञ्चित्करत्वादिति प्राहुः।

3. स्यादेतत् शब्दोऽनित्यः शब्दत्वात् इत्यत्रासाधारणेऽव्याप्तिः सर्वसाध्यवद्व्यावृत्ते-स्तत्रासत्त्वात्। एतं शब्दोऽनित्यः कृतकत्वात् इत्यस्य सत्प्रतिपक्षे नित्यत्वव्या-प्याद्रव्यद्रव्यत्वादावपि पक्षस्य तद्वत्ताविरहादित्याशङ्कां तयोरलक्ष्यत्वेन निराकुरुते दशाविशेष इति। हेत्वोः सद्धेत्वोः असाधारणः पक्षमात्रवृत्तिः सन् प्रतिपक्षो विरोधिपरामर्शो यस्य स तथा तयोर्दशाविशेषे हेतौ सर्वसाध्यवद्व्यावृत्तत्वस्य

पक्षे साध्याभावव्याप्यवत्त्वस्य च भ्रमदशायामाभासत्वात् अनुमित्यजनकत्वात्तद्धेर्हेत्वादौ साध्यवद्व्यावृत्तत्वादिबुद्धेः प्रतिबन्धकत्वं परमायाति न तु तद्विषयस्य दोषत्वम् असत्त्वात्, अन्यथा बाधभ्रमेणानुमित्यनुदयात् तस्यापि दोषत्वं स्यात्, कोहि साध्याभावतद्व्याप्यवत्ताभ्रमयोरनुमितिविरोधित्वे विशेषः, निर्युक्तिकस्तु प्रवादो न श्रद्धेयः, तत्प्रकारकप्रमाविषयत्वञ्च लक्षणार्थः, तच्च द्विविधं विषयरूपं साधारण्यादिबाधे च प्रमितसाध्याभाववान् पक्षः तद्विषयत्वेन ज्ञानस्यानुमितिप्रतिबन्धकत्वात् अविषयरूपञ्च विरोधिसामग्रीकालीनत्वादिकं तद्वत्त्वञ्च ज्ञानस्येव तद्विषयस्य हेतोरपीति, तन्न, तद्वत्त्वं हि हेतोर्नाभेदेन बाधे तदभावात्, अतएव नाश्रयतया वह्निव्यभिचारिद्रव्यत्वादिमति धूमेऽतिप्रसङ्गाच्च साध्याभाववतत्पक्षस्येव साध्याभाववद्धृत्तिहेतोर्ज्ञानस्य प्रतिबन्धकत्वात् साधारण्यादिविषयकत्वस्य ज्ञाननिष्ठस्यैव प्रतिबन्धकतावच्छेदकत्वात् सत्तादिसाध्यके ज्ञानेऽतिप्रसङ्गाच्च यथाकथञ्चित्तद्वत्त्वस्य चातिप्रसञ्जकत्वात् विरोधिसामग्रीसमवहितोऽपि च लिङ्गपरामर्शो न स्वसाध्यकानुमितेः प्रतिबन्धको मणिसमवहितो वह्निरिव दाहस्य। अथ यद्धर्मविशिष्टज्ञाने सत्यवश्यमनुमितिप्रतिवन्धः तदेवात्र प्रतिबन्धकतावच्छेदकमुक्तं, भवति च प्रतिबन्धकीभूतविरोधिसामग्रीकालीनत्वादिविशिष्टे परामर्शे तथा इति चेत् न, वैकालादिसाधारणकारणघटिता सामग्री क्वापि प्रतिबन्धिका विशेषतस्त्वत्र तत्सत्त्वे कार्य्योत्पादस्य दुर्वारत्वात् किन्तु विरोधिपरामर्शस्तथा, यदि च तत्सत्त्वेऽपि तत्साध्ये बाधावताराान्नानुमितिप्रतिबन्धः प्रामाणिकस्तदा अप्रामाण्यग्रहाभावस्येव तदभावस्यापि वैशिष्ट्यन्तत्र निवेश्यतां यथा च भ्रमप्रमासाधारणविरोधिपरामर्शसत्त्वे नानुमितिस्तथा तथाविधबाधादिग्रहेरपीत्यतिप्रसङ्गः। न चातीतादौ लिङ्गे विरोधिपरामर्शकालीनत्वमपि। यदपि तद्विषयत्वेन ज्ञानस्य अनुमितिप्रतिबन्धकत्वं तद्वत्त्वमेव वाच्यं सत्प्रतिपक्षे च विरोधिव्याप्त्यादिकमेव तथा, तद्वत्त्वमपि हेतोस्तज्ज्ञानरूपसम्बन्धेन तस्य समूहालम्बनरूपतया हेतुद्वयविषयत्वादिति तदपि तुच्छं साध्याभाववत्पक्षविषयत्वेन तादृशपक्षज्ञानप्रमात्वविषयत्वेन वा ज्ञानस्य प्रतिबन्धकत्वं, तस्य च साध्यवत्यपि पक्षे सम्भवादतिव्याप्तेः विशिष्टविषयत्वेन प्रतिबन्धकत्वं, विशिष्टञ्च तत्राप्रसिद्धमिति चेतर्हि किं सर्वत्र सत्प्रतिपक्षे साध्याभावव्याप्यवान् पक्षः प्रसिद्धः यथाकथञ्चित् सम्बन्धेन तद्वत्त्वञ्चातिप्रसक्तं धूमादेरपि ज्ञानरूपेण तदाश्रयाश्रयत्वादिना वा सम्बन्धेन व्यभिचारादिमत्त्वात् यादृशसम्बन्धावगाहित्वेन ज्ञानस्य प्रतिबन्धकत्वं तेन तद्वत्त्वञ्च न सर्वत्र सत्प्रतिपक्षिते हेतावस्ति च क्वचित् सद्धेताविति कृतं पल्लवितेन।

4. यद्यपीति, स्थाणुत्वाभावस्य तद्व्याप्यकरादेश्च निश्चये स्थाणुत्वप्रत्यक्षशाब्दयोरतुल्यत्वात्। नचैवं नरशिरः कपालं शुचि प्राण्यङ्गत्वादित्यादिनाप्यगमप्रतिरोधः स्यात्

तत्रानुकूलतर्काभावेन बलवत्तरागमविरोधेन च व्याप्तिनिश्चयस्यानुमितेश्चानुत्पत्तेरिति भाव:।

5. यद्वेत्याद्यभ्युच्चयमात्रं प्रत्यक्षं प्रत्यानुमानिकबाधादिनिश्चयस्याप्रतिबन्धकत्वेऽपि शाब्दं प्रति प्रतिबन्धकत्वात् योग्यताज्ञानेनान्यथासिद्धत्वात् तदभावो न तत्र हेतुरिति चेदेवमप्युपनीतभानविशेषं प्रति तत्त्वेन हेतुताया दुर्वारत्वात्।

APPENDIX- II

सामान्यनिरुक्तिमाथुरी

अथ हेत्वाभासनिरूपणम्

1. न्याय-तदवयवान् निरूप्य प्रसङ्गसङ्गत्या हेत्वाभासं निरूपयितुं शिष्याबधानाय प्रतिजानीते, अथेति, न्यायतदवयवयोर्निरूपणानन्तरमित्यर्थः। 'हेत्वाभासाः' आभासीभूता हेतवो दुष्टहेतवइति यावत्, हेतुवदाभासन्त इति व्युत्पत्तेः न तु हेतोराभासा दोषविशेषाः 'ते चेत्यादिना हेतुविभागानुपपत्तेः। निरूपणप्रयोजनं दर्शयति, 'तत्त्वनिर्णयेति, अवास्तवकोटिनिश्चायकहेतौ दुष्टत्वज्ञाने वास्तवकोटि-निश्चयो भवतीति तत्त्वनिर्णयप्रयोजकत्वमिति भावः। स्वार्थ-वादयोरुक्त्वा जल्प-वादयोरुक्त्वा जल्प-वितण्डयोराह, 'विजयेति, तदिदम् उद्भावनद्वारा, परोक्तहेतौ दुष्टत्वोद्भावने तस्य निग्रहादिति भावः। एवञ्च तत्त्वनिर्णयादिलक्षणैक-कार्य्यानुकूलत्वमपि प्रकृते सङ्गतिः सम्भवति, यथा हि स्वीयसन्न्यायप्रयोगे तत्त्वनिर्णयो विजयश्च तथा परकीयहेतौ दुष्टत्वोद्भावनेऽपि तत्त्वनिर्णयो विजयश्चेति बोध्यम्।

2. हेत्वाभासरूपदोषवत्त्वं दुष्टत्वमिति दुष्टहेतुलक्षणं स्फुटमेवेति तदुपेक्ष्य तद्घटकमेव दोषं लक्षयति, 'तत्रेति', 'तत्र' निरूपणे, इदं हेत्वाभासत्वं हेतुदोषत्वमित्यन्वयि, विषयत्वं सप्तम्यर्थः। 'अनुमितीति अनुमितिप्रतिबन्धकयथार्थज्ञानविषयत्वमित्यर्थः, भवति च साध्याभाववान् पक्षः साध्याभावव्याप्यवान् पक्ष इति ज्ञाने चानुमितिप्रति-बन्ध इति साध्याभाववत्पक्षरूपस्य बाधस्य साध्याभावव्याप्यवत्पक्षरूपस्य सत्प्रतिपक्षस्य हेत्वाभासत्वं, पर्वतो वह्न्यभाववात् पर्वतो वह्न्यभावव्याप्यवान् इति भ्रमादप्यनुमितिप्रतिबन्धात्तद्विषयत्वमादाय सद्धेतावतिव्याप्तिवारणाय यथार्थेति। 'यथार्थत्वञ्च सर्वांशे भ्रमिभिन्नत्वं तेनांशिकयथार्थत्वमादाय न तद्दोषतादवस्थ्यम्। न च साध्याभाववद्वृत्तिसाधनादिरूपे व्यभिचारादावव्याप्तिः तस्य व्याप्त्यादिज्ञाना-भावेनान्यथासिद्धतया अनुमित्यप्रतिबन्धकत्वादिति वाच्यं। अनुमितिपदस्य

साध्यव्याप्यहेतुमान् पक्षः साध्यवांश्चेति समूहालम्बनानुमितिपरत्वादिति भावः।

केचित्तु दुष्टहेतोरेव इदं लक्षणं। न चैवं बाधितादावव्याप्तिः तत्र हेत्वन्तर्भावेनाप्रतिबन्धकत्वादिति वाच्यम्। यथाकथञ्चित् समूहालम्वनज्ञानविषवत्व-मादायैव तत्र लक्षणसमन्वयात् न चैवमनुमितिप्रतिबन्धकसमूहालम्बनबाधादि-भ्रमविषयत्वमादाय सद्धेतावप्यतिप्रसङ्ग इति वाच्यम्। भ्रमभिन्नत्वरूपयथार्थत्वस्य विशेषणत्वेनैव तद्वारणात्। न च तथापि ह्रदो वह्निमान् इत्यनुमितिप्रतिबन्ध-कभ्रमभिन्नह्रदो धूमाभाववांश्चेति समूहालम्वनज्ञानविषयत्वमादाय पर्वतो वह्निमान् धूमादित्यादौ धूमादावतिव्याप्तिरिति वाच्यं। अनुमितिपदस्य विशिष्टप्रकृतसाध्य-व्याप्यप्रकृतहेतुमान् प्रकृतसाध्यवांश्च प्रकृतपक्ष इत्यनुमितिव्यक्तिपरत्वावश्यकत्वात्, तथाच तत्साध्यव्याप्यतद्धेतुमान् तत्साध्यवांश्च तत्पक्षइत्यनुमितिव्यक्तिप्रतिबन्ध-कभ्रमभिन्नज्ञानविषयस्तद्धेतुः तस्मिन् पक्षे तस्मिन् साध्ये दुष्टे इति विशिष्य लक्षणस्य पर्य्यवसन्नतया न कोऽपि दोषः। धूमव्याप्यवह्निमान् धूमवांश्च पर्वत इत्यनुमितिप्रतिबन्धकव्यभिचारादिज्ञानविषयस्य धूमस्य पर्वते पक्षे धूमे साध्ये दुष्टत्वाभावात् द्वितीयतद्धेतुपदं, प्रतिबन्धकता च ग्राह्याभाव-तद्व्याप्यादि-मुद्रया ग्राह्या, तेन तादृशानुमितिप्रतिबन्धकसमूहालम्बनसिद्धिविषये सद्धेतौ नातिप्रसङ्ग इति प्राहुः। तदसत्। अस्य दुष्टहेतोर्लक्षणत्वे दोषाश्रयस्य दुष्टपदार्थत्वाभावात् दुष्टपदस्य पारिभाषिकत्वापत्तेः। न च पारिभाषिकत्वमिष्टमेवेति वाच्यम्। तथासति तत्तद्धेतुत्वं तत्तत्पक्षे तत्तत्साध्ये दुष्टत्वमित्यस्यैव सम्यक्त्वेन विषयान्तर्विशेषणवैयर्थ्यापत्तेरिति दिक्।

नन्विदं व्यभिचारादिघटकसाध्यादावतिव्याप्तं तस्यापि तादृशप्रतिबन्धकव्य-भिचारादिज्ञानविषयत्वात् सिद्धेरनुमितिप्रबिन्धकतया साध्यवत्पक्षे चातिव्याप्तिः। न च यादृशविशिष्टविषयकत्वं तादृशानुमितिप्रतिबन्धकतानतिरिक्तवृत्ति तादृशविशिष्टत्वं हेत्वाभासत्वम्। भवति च साध्याभावविशिष्टपक्ष-साध्याभाववद्वृत्तित्वविशिष्टसाधनादिविषयकत्वं तथेति वाच्यम्। 'यथार्थत्वस्य वैयर्थ्यप्रसङ्गात्। भ्रमविषयविशिष्टस्याप्रसिद्धत्वादित्यरुचेर्यथार्थत्वविशेषणं परित्यज्य लक्षणान्तरमाह, 'यद्विषयत्वेनेति, 'लिङ्गज्ञानस्येत्यत्र लिङ्गमविवक्षितं बाधादिज्ञानस्य लिङ्गाविषयकत्वात् व्यर्थत्वाच्च। 'अनुमितिपदञ्च साध्यव्याप्यहेतुमान् पक्षः साध्यवान् इत्यनुमितिपरम्, अन्यथोक्तक्रमेण [illegible]व्याप्तिः। तथाच यद्विषयकत्वेन ज्ञानस्य धूमव्याप्यवह्निमान् पर्वतो धूमवान्, इत्यनुमितिप्रतिबन्धकत्वं स पर्वतत्वरूपेण पक्षतायां धूमत्वरूपेण साध्यतायां वह्नित्वरूपेण पक्षतायां धूमत्वरूपेण साध्यतायां वह्नित्वरूपेण हेतुतायां दोष इति प्रातिस्विकरूपेणैव लक्षणम् अन्यथा साध्यादेरननुगमेन एकतरोपादानेऽन्यत्राव्याप्त्यापत्तेः, पर्वतो वह्निमान् धूमादित्यादावपि पर्वतादौ काञ्चनयत्वाभावादेर्दोषत्वापत्तेश्च तज्ज्ञानस्यापि

काञ्चनमयः पर्वतो वह्निमान् धूमादित्यनुमितिप्रतिबन्धकत्वात्। नन्विदमपि पक्षसाध्यादावतिव्याप्तं तस्याप्यवच्छेदककोटिप्रविष्टत्वात्। न च यत्विषयतासम्बन्धेनानुमितिप्रतिबन्धकतावच्छेदकतायाः पर्य्याप्त्यधिकरणं तत्त्वमर्थइति वाच्यं। तथा सति साध्याभाववत्पक्षादेरप्यदोषत्वापत्तेः न हि साध्याभाववत्पक्षादिविषयकनिश्चयत्वेनानुमितिप्रतिबन्धकत्वं, विशिष्टस्यानतिरिक्ततया केवलपक्षादिविषयकज्ञानादेरपि प्रतिबन्धकत्वापत्तेः।

अथ यद्विशेष्यक-यत्प्रकारकनिश्चयत्वेनानुमितिप्रतिबन्धकता तद्विशिष्टतत्त्वं दोषत्वं, भवति च पक्षविशेष्यक-साध्याभावप्रकारकनिश्चयत्वेन साधनविशेय्यक-साध्याभाववद्वृत्तित्वप्रकारकनिश्चयत्वादिना च प्रतिवन्धकतेति साध्याभाववत्पक्षः साध्याभाववद्वृत्तिसाधनादिर्दोषइति चेत्। न। प्रतिबन्धकता हि न पक्षविशेष्यकसाध्याभावप्रकारकनिश्चयत्वेन प्रमेयवान्, पक्ष इति ज्ञानेऽपि प्रतिबन्धापत्तेः, न वा साध्याभावत्वरूपेण साध्याभावप्रकारकनिश्चयवत्त्वेन पक्षे साध्यप्रतियोगिकत्वेन घटाभावाद्यवगाहिभ्रमस्य साध्याभावत्वरूपेण घटाद्यवगाहि-भ्रमस्य चाप्रतिबन्धकत्वापत्तेः, किन्तु अभावत्वरूपेण यत्किञ्चिद्वस्तुनि साध्य-प्रकारकः पक्षे चाभावत्वरूपेण यत्किञ्चिद्वस्तुप्रकारको यो निश्चयः तत्त्वेन तथात्वम्। न चैवमपि साध्याभाववान् अभाववांश्च पक्ष इति समूहालम्बनज्ञानादपि प्रतिबन्धापत्तिरिति वाच्यम्। विलक्षणविषयताकतादृशनिश्चयत्वेन प्रतिबन्धकत्वादिति। अत्राहुः यद्विषयत्वेनेत्यत्रानतिरिक्तवृत्तित्वाख्यमवच्छेदकत्वं तृतीयार्थो न तु स्वरूपसम्बन्धविशेषः पक्षसाध्यादिविषयत्वञ्च न तथेति नातिप्रसङ्गः, साध्याभावविशिष्टपक्षादिविषयकत्वन्तु तथेति तेषां दोषत्वम्। अथ तथापि ह्रदविशेष्यकत्वावच्छिन्नवह्न्यभावत्वविशिष्टवह्न्यभावनिरूपितप्रकारिताव्यक्तेः वह्न्यभावप्रकारकत्वावच्छिन्नह्रदत्वविशिष्टह्रदनिरूपितविशेष्यिताव्यक्तेश्च ह्रदो वह्निमान् इत्यनुमितिप्रतिबन्धकतानतिरिक्तवृत्तितया केवलवह्न्यभावत्वविशिष्टवह्न्यभावे केवलह्रदत्वविशिष्टह्रदे चातिव्याप्तिर्दुर्वारा। न च केवलवह्न्य-भावादिर्लक्ष्य एव, तन्मात्रे हेत्वाभासव्यवहाराभावेन साध्याभाववत्पक्षादेरेव तथात्वात् तन्मात्रस्य दोषत्वे पर्वतो वह्निमान् धूमादित्यादेरपि दुष्टत्वापत्तेः येन केनचित् सम्बन्धेन दोषवत एव दुष्टत्वादिति चेत्। न। यद्विषयितासामान्यं तादृशानुमितिप्रतिबन्धकतानतिरिक्तवृत्ति तत्त्वस्य विवक्षितत्वात्, केवलवह्न्यभावत्वविशिष्टवह्न्यभावादिविषयितासामान्यन्तु न तथा, तद्विषयत्वस्य वह्निर्नास्तीत्युच्छृङ्खलज्ञानेऽपि सत्त्वात्। न चैवं विशिष्टस्यानतिरिक्ततया केवलह्रदादिविषयकज्ञाने प्रमेयवान् प्रमेयमित्यादिज्ञाने च वह्न्यभावादिविशिष्टह्रदादिविषयकत्वसत्त्वादसम्भव इति वाच्यं। यद्विषयित्वपदस्य यादृशविशिष्ट-

विषयित्वपरत्वात्, विशिष्टविषयित्वञ्च विशिष्टनिरूपितं विषयित्वं, तस्य च विलक्षणस्य वह्न्यभाववान् ह्रद इत्यादिप्रमात्मकज्ञान एव सत्त्वेन केवलह्रदादिविषयकज्ञाने अभावात्। अतएव सिद्धिविषयीभूतसाध्यवत्पक्षेऽपि नातिव्याप्तिः यद्विषयकत्वस्य सिषाधयिषाकालीनसाध्यनिश्चयेऽपि सत्त्वेन प्रतिबन्धकतातिरिक्तवृत्तित्वात्, तद्व्यावृत्तप्रतिबन्धकताया विवक्षणाद्वा। यादृशविशिष्टविषयित्वञ्चाव्याप्यवृत्तित्वज्ञानानास्कन्दितागृहीताप्रामाण्यकनिश्चयनिष्ठत्वेन विशेषणीयं, तेन तस्येच्छादौ संशयेऽव्याप्यवृत्तित्वज्ञानास्कन्दितनिश्चये गृहीताप्रामाण्यकनिश्चये च सत्त्वेऽपि नासम्भवः। न चैवं वृक्षः संयोगी द्रव्यत्वादित्याद्यव्याप्यवृत्तिसाध्यके संयोगाभाववद्वृक्षादावतिव्याप्तिः अव्याप्यवृत्तित्वग्रहानास्कन्दितागृहीताप्रामाण्यकनिश्चयनिष्ठतादृशविशिष्टविषयित्वस्याप्यनुमितिप्रतिबन्धकतानतिरिक्तवृत्तित्वादिति वाच्यम्। तस्य बाधस्वरूपत्वेन लक्ष्यत्वात् "बाधेऽपक्षधर्म्मो हेतुरनैकान्तिको वा" इति प्रवादस्य व्याप्यवृत्तिसाध्यकबाधपरत्वात्। न च तस्य बाधत्वे सद्धेतोरपि तस्य बाधितत्वापत्तिरिति वाच्यं हेत्वाभासविभाजकतावच्छेदकस्य बाधितत्वस्य तत्रेष्टत्वात् बाधितत्वव्यवहारनियामके तु निरवच्छिन्नाऽधिकरणतासम्बन्धेन साध्याभाववत्त्वस्य घटकत्वात्। न चैवं वृक्षः संयोगी द्रव्यत्वादित्यादावेव बाधस्य स्वरूपासिद्धिव्यभिचारासङ्कीर्णोदाहरणतया किं तस्य उदाहरणान्तरगवेषणयेति वाच्यम् अशोकवनिकान्यायात् अतिस्फुटतया ग्रन्थकर्त्तुरुपेक्षणात्। अथैवं प्रमेयत्वादिविशिष्टवह्न्यभाववद्ह्रदाद्यात्मकस्य विशिष्टस्यापि दोषत्वापत्तिः तद्विषयित्वस्यापि प्रतिबन्धकतानतिरिक्तवृत्तित्वात्। न च तादृशविशिष्टान्तराघटितत्वेन यादृशविशिष्टं विशेषणीयं उक्तविशिष्टन्तु न तथा तस्य तादृशविशिष्टान्तरेण वह्न्यभाववद्ह्रदादिना घटितत्वादिति वाच्यम्। प्रमेयत्वम् अवृत्ति प्रमेयत्वादित्यादाववृत्तित्वाभाववद्वृत्तिप्रमेयत्वादिरूपे व्यभिचारेऽव्याप्तिः तस्य वृत्तिप्रमेयत्वरूपबाधघटितत्वादिति चेत्। न। स्वानिरूपितविशिष्टविशेष्यकत्वानवच्छेद्यत्वेन प्रतिबन्धकताविशेषणात्, स्वपदं लक्ष्यत्वाभिमतविशिष्टपरं, प्रमेयत्वादिविशिष्टवह्न्यभाववद्ह्रदात्मकविशिष्टन्तु न तथा, तद्विषयकत्वावच्छिन्नप्रतिबन्धकतायाः स्वानिरुपितेन केवलवह्न्यभाववद्ह्रदविशेष्यकत्वेनाप्यवच्छिन्नतात्, स्वानिरूपितविशिष्टविशेष्यकत्वानवच्छिन्नत्वञ्च स्वानिरूपितविशिष्टविशेष्यकत्वानतिरिक्तवृत्तिकप्रतिबन्धकताभिन्नत्वम्। न चैवं प्रतियोगिब्यधिकरणत्वविशिष्टसाध्याभाववत्[illegible] [illegible] [illegible]: तद्विषयकत्वावच्छिन्नप्रतिबन्धकतायाः स्वानिरूपितेन केवलसाध्याभाववत्पक्षविशेष्यकत्वेनाप्यवच्छिन्नत्वादिति वाच्यम्। केवलसाध्याभाववत्पक्षस्यैव बाधताया तस्याबाधत्वात् अयं वृक्षः कपिसंयोगी

तत्त्वादित्यादावपि बाधस्येष्टत्वात्। न च तथाप्यनुमितिपदस्य यथोक्तसमूहालम्बनानुमितिपरतया निर्वह्निः पर्वतो वह्निमान् वह्निव्यभिचारिधर्म्मादित्यादौ न कोऽप्याभासः स्यात्तत्र यथोक्तसमूहालम्बनानुमितेरप्रसिद्धेरिति वाच्यम्। निर्वह्निमान् इत्यादिवन्निर्वह्निः पर्वतो वह्निमान् वह्निव्यभिचारिधर्म्भादित्यादेरप्यपार्थकतया तत्र हेत्वाभासविरहेऽपि क्षतिविरहात्। यद्वा प्रकृतपक्षतावच्छेदकरूपेण प्रकृतपक्षे प्रकृतसाध्यताबच्छेदकरूपेण प्रकृतसाध्यवैशिष्ट्यावगाहिनी सती प्रकृतसाध्यतावच्छेदकरूपेण प्रकृतसाध्यनिरूपितव्याप्तिप्रकारेण प्रकृतहेतुतावच्छेदकरूपेण प्रकृतेहतुवैशिष्ट्यावगाहिनी या बुद्धिः सा यत्र यदवगाहते तत्र तद्वैशिष्ट्यावगाहि यज्ज्ञानं तत्प्रतिबन्धकतानतिरिक्तवृत्ति यादृशविशिष्टनिरूपितविषयितासामान्यं तादृशविशिष्टत्वं हेतुदोषत्वमिति विवक्षणीयम्। इत्थञ्च वह्न्यभाववत्पर्वतादेरेव तत्र दोषत्वं तद्विषयकनिश्चयमात्रस्यैव निर्वह्निः पर्वतो वह्निमानित्यादिज्ञानं यत्र यदवगाहते तत्र तदवगाहिनः केवलपर्वतो वह्निमानित्यनाहार्य्यज्ञानस्य प्रतिबन्धकत्वात्। न च तादृशबुद्धेरेव उक्तस्थलेऽप्रसिद्धिरिति वाच्यम्। आहार्य्यरूपस्य तस्य सम्भवात्। न चैवं पर्वतो वह्निमान् इत्यादौ काञ्चनमयत्वाभाववत्पर्वतादेरपि दोषत्वं स्यात् तद्विषयकनिश्चयस्य पर्वतो वह्निमानित्यादिज्ञानं यत्र यदवगाहते तत्र तदवगाहिनः काञ्चनमयः पर्वतो वह्निमानित्यादिज्ञानस्य प्रतिबन्धकत्वादिति वाच्यम्। तत्र तदवगाहित्वांशे प्रतिबन्धकताया विवक्षितत्वादिति संक्षेपः। इदन्तु चिन्त्यं यत्र क्षेत्रविशेषादौ यदङ्कुरविशेषस्य ज्ञानं कस्यापि न जातं तत्र क्षेत्रविशेषादौ प्रमेयत्वादिना तदङ्कुरविशेषादौ साध्ये न कोऽप्याभासः स्यात् तत्र तादृशबुद्धेरप्रसिद्धेः। न च तत्राभासो नेष्ट एव, व्यवहारादेरविशेषेणानिच्छायाः स्वातन्त्र्यमात्रत्वात्। किञ्च यदङ्कुरविशेषस्य वह्न्यभाववत्पर्वतादिविषयक एव निश्चयो जातः न तु कदाचिदपि तदविषयस्तन्निश्चयः तदङ्कुरविशेषस्य पर्वतो वह्निमानित्यादौ दोषत्वापत्तेरिति दिक्।

इदमत्रावधेयं बाधादिविषयतानियतविषयिताके तदङ्कुरादिव्यक्तिविशेषे यथाविवक्षितलक्षणस्य नातिप्रसङ्गशङ्कापि तादृशज्ञाननिष्ठतथाविधानुमितिप्रतिबन्धकतायां बाधादिविषयकत्वरूपेण विशिष्टविषयकत्वान्तरेणावच्छिन्नत्वात्, मेयत्वविशिष्टबाधादावतिप्रसङ्गवारणाय ग्रन्थकृतैव पूर्वं विशिष्टविषयकत्वान्तरानवच्छेद्यत्वेन प्रतिबन्धकताया विशेषितत्वात्। न च तादृशज्ञाननिष्ठबाधादिविषयिता तदङ्कुरादिविषयिता चैकैवेति वक्तुं शक्यते, निरूपकभेदेन विषयिताभेदस्य सिद्धान्तसिद्धत्वात्। न च पर्वतो वह्निमान् धूमादित्यादिसद्धेतावेव बाधादिभ्रममात्रविषयीभूताङ्कुरादिविशेषे विवक्षितलक्षणस्याप्यतिव्याप्तिरिति शङ्कनीयं,

तदङ्कुरादिविशेषस्यान्ततो भगवज्ज्ञानादिविषयता तथाविधभ्रमविषयमात्रविषयत्वा-सम्भवात्। न च तथापि बाधादिभ्रम-नित्यज्ञानोभयमात्रविषये व्यक्तिविशेषेऽतिव्याप्तिरितिवाच्यम्। तादृशव्यक्तिविषयिताया नित्यज्ञानेऽपि सत्त्वेन तत्र तदनुमितिप्रतिबन्धकताविरहात्। न च सिद्धिविधया तत्रापि तदनुमितिप्रतिबन्धकत्वं, नित्यज्ञाने सिषाधयिषाविरहवैशिष्ट्यविरहेण सिद्धिप्रतिबन्धकत्वस्यापि तत्रासम्भवात्। न च यत्र तदङ्कुरो वह्न्यभाववानित्येव बाधज्ञानं तत्र तादृशबाध-ज्ञानमात्रविषये तदङ्कुरत्वविशिष्टेऽतिव्याप्तिरिति वाच्यम्। तत्र प्रकृतपक्षे साध्यवैशिष्ट्यावगाहिज्ञानाप्रसिद्ध्यातिव्याप्त्यनवकाशात्। न च यत्र तदङ्कुरो वह्निमानित्यनुमितिरपि प्रसिद्धा तत्रैवातिव्याप्तिरिति वाच्यम्। तत्र तद्विषयकत्वस्य तादृशानुमितावपि सत्त्वेन तत्र तादृशानुमितिप्रतिबन्धकत्वविरहात् सिद्धिविधया प्रतिबन्धकत्वस्यापि प्रागुत्तरवर्त्तिसिषाधयिषाकज्ञानेऽभावात्। यदि च नैतादृशं सिषाधयिषासमवहितं तज्ज्ञानं कदापि जातमित्युच्यते, तदा तु सिद्धिविशेष-विषयेऽतिप्रसङ्गवारणाय सिद्धिविधया प्रतिबन्धकतातिरिक्तप्रतिबन्धकतैव लक्षणे निवेशनीया, तथाच कुतोऽयमतिप्रसङ्ग इति दिक्।

यत्तु यत्र बाधादिविषयतानियतविषयिताकोऽङ्कुरादिव्यक्तिविशेषस्तत्र बाधादाव्याप्तिस्तत्र तदनुमितिप्रतिबन्धकतया अङ्कुरादिव्यक्तिविशेषविषयत्वरूपेण विशिष्टविषयकत्वान्तरेणावच्छेद्यत्वात् इति, तन्न, विशिष्टविषयकत्वान्त-रानवच्छेद्येत्यत्र स्वरूपसम्बन्धरूपावच्छेद्यत्वस्यैव विशेषणीयत्वात्। वस्तुतो वह्न्यभाववद्ह्रदवत्प्रमेयत्वविषयित्वावच्छेद्यतया असम्भववारणाय स्वघटिता-निरूपितविशिष्टविशेष्यकत्वानवच्छेद्यत्वं विवक्षणीयं, स्वघटितत्वञ्च स्वाविषयकप्रतीत्यविषयत्वं, तथाच तदङ्कुरादेर्बाधादिघटिततया बाधादेः स्वघटितानिरूपितविशिष्टविशेष्यकत्वावच्छेद्यप्रतिबन्धकतानतिरिक्तवृत्तित्वादन्यून-वृत्तित्वरूपावच्छेद्यत्वनिवेशेऽपि न क्षतिरिति मन्तव्यम्।

यन्मते ज्ञायमानलिङ्गस्य करणत्ववत् ज्ञायमानव्यभिचारादेरपि प्रतिबधकत्वं तन्मते लक्षणमाह, 'ज्ञायमानमिति, अत्रापि, 'अनुमितिपदं प्रकृतपक्षतावच्छेदक-रूपेण प्रकृतसाध्यावगाहिनी सती प्रकृतसाध्यतावच्छेदकरूपेण प्रकृतसाध्य-निपरूपितव्याप्तिप्रकारेण प्रकृतहेतुतावच्छेदकरूपेण प्रकृतहेतुवैशिष्ट्यावगाहिनी या बुद्धिस्तत्परं, तेन व्यभिचारादनुमित्यप्रतिबन्धकत्वेऽपि नाव्याप्तिः, प्रतिबन्ध-कत्वञ्च तादृशी बुद्धिर्यत्र यदवगाहते तत्र तदवगाहिज्ञानप्रतिबन्धकत्वं वक्तव्यं, तेन निर्वह्निः पर्व्वतो वह्निमानित्यादौ नोक्तरीत्या आभासासम्भवः एवमन्यदप्युक्तदिशावसेयम्। अथैतेषु लक्षणेषु अज्ञानपक्षतावच्छेदकरूपा-सिद्ध्यादावव्याप्तिः तत्र तत्र प्रतिबन्धकत्वे ज्ञानानुपयोगात्। न च तदलक्ष्यमेव,

एकविंशतिनिग्रहस्थानवहिर्भूतस्य तस्य हेत्वाभासमध्येऽप्यनन्तर्भावे निग्रहस्थानत्वानुपपत्तेः न चानुक्तसमुच्चयपरेण चरमसूत्रस्थचकारेण तस्यापि समुच्चयान्निग्रहस्थानत्वव्यवस्थितिरिति वाच्यम्। तथासति निग्रहस्थानस्य द्वाविंशतिप्रभेदत्वानुपपत्तेरिति चेत्। न। निग्रहस्थानत्वौपयिकस्य हेत्वाभासत्वस्य पृथगेव निर्वक्ष्यमाणत्वादिह तु हेतुदोषा निरूप्यन्त इति न काप्यनुपपन्तिः, येन केनचित् सम्बन्धेन तु दुष्टत्वम्। न चैव सद्धेतावतिव्याप्तिः वह्न्यभाववद्वृत्तिजलत्वादेर्येन केनापि सम्बन्धेन धूमादिनिष्ठत्वादिति वाच्यम्। तत्पक्षक-तत्साध्यक-तद्धेतुको यो दोषः येन केनापि सम्बन्धेन तद्वान् स हेतुः तस्मिन् साध्ये पक्षे दुष्ट इति विवक्षितत्वादित्यास्तां विस्तरः।

3. ननु साध्यव्यापकीभूताभावप्रतियोगिहेतुमत्पक्षरूपस्यासाधारणत्वस्य साध्याभावव्याप्यवत्पक्षरूपस्य सत्प्रतिपक्षस्य च धियोऽनुमितिप्रतिबन्धकत्वे मानाभावः ग्रह्याभावाद्यनवगाहित्वात् इत्यत आह 'दशाविशेषे हेत्वोरेवेति, 'एवकारो भिन्नक्रमे, असाधारणसत्प्रतिपक्षयोर्हेत्वोर्दशाविशेष एव सत्प्रतिपक्षासाधारणत्वेन भानदशायामेव, 'आभासत्वात्' अनुमित्यजनकत्वादित्यर्थः, एवकारेण तदज्ञानदशायान्तु जननादिति सूचितं, तथाचान्वयव्यतिरेकात् तज्ज्ञानस्य प्रतिबन्धकत्वमिति भावः।

4. नन्वेतानि लक्षणानि बाधसत्प्रतिपक्षयोरतिव्याप्तानि अनुमित्यसाधारणदोषस्यैवात्र लक्ष्यत्वात् तयोश्च प्रत्यक्ष-शाब्दज्ञानयोरपि प्रतिबन्धकतया साधारणत्वादिति केषाञ्चिद् दूषणमपाकरोति, 'यद्यपीत्यादिना, न लिङ्गाभासत्वं, न लिङ्गासाधारणदोषत्वं नानुमित्यसाधारणदोषत्वमिति यावत्, ज्ञायमानस्याभासस्येति विशिष्टबुद्धिसामान्यप्रतिबन्धकज्ञानविषयस्य दोषमात्रस्येत्यर्थः, तथाच तयोरपि लक्ष्यत्वान्नातिव्याप्तिरिति भावः।

अत्र केचित् शाब्दे बाधज्ञानमात्रं न प्रतिबन्धकं नरशिरःकपालं शुचि प्राण्यङ्गत्वात् शङ्खवदत्यनुमानेन ''मल-मूत्र-पुरीषास्थिनिर्गतं ह्यशुचि स्मृतम्। नारं स्पृष्ट्वा तु सस्नेहं सचेलोजलमाविशेत्'' इति वेदबाधापत्तेः किन्तु अनुमित्यन्यबाधज्ञानत्वेन। न चैवं परमाणुरनित्य इति शब्दस्यापि ज्ञानजनकत्वापत्तिः परमाणुर्नित्यः जन्यमहत्त्वानधिकरणत्वे सति द्रव्यत्वादित्यनुमितेरप्रतिबन्धकत्वाद् बाधज्ञानान्तरस्य चाभावादिति वाच्यम्। अगृहीतविशेषेत्यनेनानुमितिविशेषणात् तत्र च प्रामाण्यग्रह एवानुमितौ विशेष इत्याहुः तन्न, शब्दबुद्धित्वावच्छिन्नं प्रति तेन रूपेण पृथक्प्रतिबन्धकत्वान्तरकल्पने गौरवान्मानाभावाच्च। न च यथोक्तानुमानादशौचबोधकवेदबाधापत्तिरेव मानं, तत्रानुकूलतर्काभावेनागमविरोधेन च व्याप्तिनिश्चयस्यानुमितेश्चानुत्पत्तेरनुमित्युत्पत्तौ च प्रतिबन्धकत्वस्येष्टत्वादिति।

5. नन्वनुमाननिरूपणप्रस्तावे प्रमाणसामान्यदोषाभिधानमनुचितमित्यनुशयेनाह, 'यद्वेति, 'बाधेनेति परोक्षबाधनिश्चयेनेत्यर्थः, परोक्षसत्प्रतिपक्षेण चेत्यपि बोध्यं, आनुमानिक-

बाध-तद्व्याप्यवत्तादिज्ञानसत्त्वेऽपि लौकिकविशिष्टसाक्षात्कारोदयात्। न चैतावतापि शाब्दबोधे तत्प्रतिबन्धकत्वमस्त्येवेति वाच्यम्। योग्यताज्ञानेनान्यथासिद्धतया शाब्दबोधं प्रति बाध-तद्व्याप्यवत्तादिज्ञानमात्रस्यैवाप्रतिबन्धकत्वादिति भावः। 'अनुमिताविति, तथाच बाधनिश्चयत्वादिसामान्यरूपेण प्रतिबन्धकत्वास्यानुमितिं प्रत्येव सत्त्वात्तेन रूपेणासाधारणदोषत्वमस्त्येवेति भावः। इदञ्चापाततः, लौकिकप्रत्यक्षनिश्चये आनुमानिकबाधादिनिश्चयसामान्यस्याप्रतिबन्धकत्वेऽपि संशयोपनीतभानं प्रति तस्य प्रतिबन्धकतया बाधनिश्चयत्वादिरूपेणाप्य-साधारणत्वविरहात्। न चोपनीतभानं प्रत्यपि बाधनिश्चयत्वादिना न प्रतिबन्ध-कत्वमपि तु इच्छाविशेषादिविरहविशिष्टबाधनिश्चयवत्त्वादिनैव बाध-निश्चयसत्त्वऽप्याहार्य्योपनीतभानोदयादिति वाच्यम्। तथापि स्मृत्युपमितीं प्रति बाधनिश्चत्वादिना बाधनिश्चयसामान्यस्यैव प्रतिबन्धकतया असाधारण्यविरहादिति ध्येयम्।

असिद्ध-विरूद्ध सव्यभिचारानध्यवसिताश्चत्वारो हेत्वाभासाः, अनध्यवसि-तोऽसाधारणः न तु बाध-प्रतिरोधौ हेत्वाभासाविति वैशेषिकसिद्धान्तस्तन्निराकरणाय स्वमतसिद्धान् हेत्वाभासान् विभजते,' 'ते चेति, आभासीभूता हेतव इति षेषः। 'सव्यभिचारेति व्यभिचारात्मकेन दोषेण सह वर्त्तत इति व्युत्पत्त्या व्यभिचारीत्यर्थः व्यभिचारित्वरूपञ्चानुपदमेव विवेचयिष्यते। 'विरूद्धेति साध्यासमानाधिकरणो हेतुर्विरोधः, तादात्म्येन तद्वान् हेतुर्विरूद्धः, एतज्जानञ्च साध्यसामानाधिकरण्य-घटितव्याप्तिप्रकारकज्ञाने सामानाधिकरण्यांशे प्रतिबन्धकम्, उदाहरणन्तु समवायेन साध्यहेतुको गोत्ववानश्वत्वादित्यादिरिति मणिकृतः।

प्राञ्चस्तु साध्यासामानाधिकरण्यं विरोधः तद्वान् हेतुर्विरूद्ध इत्याहुः। तदसत्। केवलसाध्यासामानाधिकरण्यरूपविशिष्टनिरूपितविषयित्वस्य केवलसाध्या-सामानाधिकरण्यविषयकज्ञाने हेत्वन्तरविशेष्यकतत्प्रकारकज्ञाने च सत्त्वेन प्रकृतहेतुकानुमितितत्कारणज्ञानप्रतिबन्धकतातिरिक्तवृत्तितया केवलस्य तस्य हेतुदोषत्वासम्भवात्, अतएवाग्रेऽपि सर्वत्र विशेष्यान्तर्भाव इति मन्तव्यम्। 'सत्प्रतिपक्षेति सत्प्रतिपक्षपदस्य नीलादिपदवद्धर्मधर्म्युभयवाचकत्वात् सत्प्रतिपक्षित इत्यर्थः, साध्याभावव्याप्यवान् पक्षः सत्प्रतिपक्षः वृत्तिमत्त्वादियथा-कथञ्चित्सम्बन्धेन तद्वान् हेतुः सत्प्रतिपक्षितः, एतज्ज्ञानञ्च साक्षादेवानुमितिविरोधि, तदभावनिश्चयवत्तदभावव्याप्यनिश्चयस्यापि तद्विशिष्टबुद्धिप्रतिबन्धकत्वात्, उदाहरणन्तु ह्रदो वह्निमान् धूमादित्यादिबाधितमात्रमेव, सद्धेतुस्तु कदाचिदपि न सत्प्रतिपक्षितः। बाधितस्तु कदापि नासत्प्रतिपक्षितः इति तु नव्याः।

प्राञ्चस्तु समानबलप्रकृतपक्षविशेष्यकसाध्याभावव्याप्यवत्त्वपरामर्शकालीन-प्रकृतपक्षविशेष्यकः-साध्यव्याप्यवत्त्वपरामर्शः सत्प्रतिपक्षः विषयतासम्बन्धेन

तद्वान् हेतुः सत्प्रतिपक्षितः, अयञ्च स्वरूपसन्नेव साक्षादनुमितिविरोधी, अत एव सद्धेतुरपि साध्याभावव्याप्यवत्तापराभर्शकाले सत्प्रतिपक्षितः बाधितोऽपि तदभावदशायां कदाचिदसत्प्रतिपक्षित इत्याहुः। एतन्मते यथोक्तं न दोषलक्षणं किन्तु दुष्टलक्षणमेवेति न तत्राव्याप्तिः।

'असिद्धेति, असिद्धः त्रिबिधः स्वरूपासिद्धः आश्रयासिद्धो व्याप्यत्वासिद्धश्च। तत्र हेत्वभाववान् पक्षः स्वरूपासिद्धिः कालिकादियत्किञ्चित्सम्बन्धेन तद्वान् हेतुः, स्वरूपासिद्धः एतज्ज्ञानञ्च पक्षधर्म्मतांशे परामर्शविरोधि, उदाहरणन्तु ह्रदो वह्निमान् धूमादित्यादि। पक्षविशेषणासिद्धिराश्रयासिद्धिः सा च पक्षतावच्छेदकाभाववान् पक्षः वृत्तिमत्त्वादियत्किञ्चित्सम्बन्धेन हेतोस्तद्वत्त्वं, एतज्ज्ञानञ्च पक्षतावच्छेदकवैशिष्ट्यांशे अनुमितिपरामर्शयोरुभयोरेव विराधि, उदाहरणन्तु काञ्चनमयः पर्व्वतो वह्निमान् इत्यादि। व्याप्यत्वासिद्धिः त्रिविधा साध्यविशेषणासिद्धिः हेतुविशेषणासिद्धिः व्याप्त्यभावरूपासिद्धिश्च, तत्र साध्यतावच्छेदकाभाववत्साध्यं साध्यविशेषणासिद्धिः सामानाधिकरण्यादियत्कि-ञ्चित्सम्बन्धेन हेतोस्तद्वत्त्वं, एतज्ज्ञानञ्च साध्यतावच्छेदक-वैशिष्ट्यांशेऽनुमिति-परामर्शयोर्विरोधि, उदाहरणन्तु पर्व्वतः काञ्चनमयवह्निमानित्यादि। हेतुतावच्छेद-काभाववान् हेतुः हेतुविशेषणासिद्धिः, तादात्म्यसम्बन्धेन हेतोस्तद्वत्त्वं, एतज्ज्ञानं हेतौ हेतुतावच्छेदकवैशिष्ट्यांशे परामर्शविरोधि, उदाहरणन्तु पर्वतो वह्निमान् काञ्चनमयधूमादित्या व्याप्त्यभाववान् हेतुर्व्याप्यत्वासिद्धिः तादात्म्येन तद्वान् हेतुर्व्याप्यत्वासिद्धः, एतज्ज्ञानञ्च हेतौ व्याप्तिज्ञानविरोधि, उदाहरणन्तु व्यभिचारिमात्रमेव। 'बाधितेति, साध्याभाववान् पक्षो बाधः, वृत्तिमत्तादियत्किञ्चि-त्सम्बन्धेन तद्वान् हेतुः बाधितः, एतज्ज्ञानञ्च साक्षादेवानुमितिविरोधि, उदाहरणन्तु ह्रदो वह्निमान् धूमादित्यादीति संक्षेपतः सामान्यतो दूषकतावीजनिर्णयः, विशेषतस्तु तत्तद्ग्रन्थ एव विवेचयिष्माम इति दिक्।

इति श्रीमथुरानाथतर्कवागीश-विरचिते तत्त्वचिन्तामणिरहस्ये अनुमानाख्यद्वितीय-खण्डरहस्ये हेत्वाभासे हेत्वाभाससामान्यनिरुक्तिरहस्यम्।

Glossary

अतिप्रसक्ति, अतिप्रसङ्ग, अतिव्याप्ति—Over-applicability, unwanted over-extension, being too wide, over-extension.

अत्यन्ताभव—absolute non-existence.

अनुगतरूप—underlying common attribute.

अन्योन्याश्रय—fault of mutual dependence.

अन्वय—process of agreement.

अन्वयव्याप्ति—universal concomitance ascertained by the process of agreement.

अन्वयिहेतु—a reason known to be concomitant by the process of agreement only.

अवच्छेदक—determinant attribute, delimiting factor/attribute.

अबाधित—uncontradicted.

असिद्धत्व—nature of being unfounded.

अव्याप्ति—being too narrow, fault of being less extensive, under-extension.

अभिव्यञ्जक—indicator.

अभेदानुमान—inference of identity.

असत्प्रतिपक्षितत्व—uncounterbalanced.

आकाङ्क्षा—expectancy.

आक्षेप—implication.

आपत्ति—objection, imposition.

आभास—fault, unreal appearance.

इष्टापत्ति—favourable objection.

उदाहरण—illustration, example.

उदासीनवाक्य—neutral sentence, indifferent sentence.

उपनीतभान—cognition produced by super-normal relation.

उपनय—assimilation.

उपस्थिति—knowldege, appearance in cognition.

उद्देश्यानुमिति—inference of the middleman caused by the verbal cognition of five constituent sentences of syllogism. Inference caused by the concerned subject and the probandum.

औपयिक—suitable means, expedient, fit.

कण्टकोद्धार—refutation of counter-arguments.

कथा—debate.

गमकत्व—capacity of being indicative.

छल—trick.

जाति—universal, genus, retort.

जातिसङ्कर—overlapping of universals, mutual encroachment of two universals.

जिज्ञासा—desire of knowing.

तान्त्रिकव्यवहार—use in the manuals of sciences.

तृतीयलिङ्गपरामर्श—synthetic consideration of the reason for the third time.

निगमन—conclusion.

निग्रहस्थान—conditions for defeat.

नियत—invariable, constant.

निवर्तक—remover.

निर्विकल्पकज्ञान—non-propositional awareness.

न्याय—inferential syllogism, inferential judgement.

न्यायाङ्ग—constituent of syllogism or judgement.

पक्ष—subject of inference.

पक्षधर्मता—property of being present in the subject.

परार्थानुमान—inference for others, inferential syllogism.

परामर्श—synthetic ascertainment of the reason, consideration.

पर्य्याप्ति—sufficiency, entireness.

प्रकार—character, feature, specification.

प्रतिज्ञा—declaration.

प्रतिवादी—opponent.

प्रतियोगी—counter-correlate, counter-positive

प्रत्यक्ष—perception, means of perception.

प्रयोजक—cause, one which effects.

प्रयोजन—necessity.

वादी—proponent.

वाह्यकरण—exernal instrument.

विपक्ष—dissimilar instance.

विप्रतिपत्ति—objection, opposition of opinion.

विभक्ति—disjoining, grammatical suffix.

विशेषण—adjective, attribute.

विषय—content or object of knowledge.

विशिष्टवैशिष्ट्य—qualification of something qualified, qualified characteristics.

विशेषलक्षण—specific definition/attribute.

विशेष्य—substantive.

वीप्सा—desire for repetition.

विषयता—objectivity.

विषयिता—subjectivity.

व्याप्ति—pervasion, coverage, universal concomitance.

विपर्य्यास—inverted order.

व्यतिरेक्युदाहरण—reverse illustration.

व्यासज्यवृत्ति—inherent in conglomeration.

व्यतिरेकव्याप्ति—universal concomitance known by the process of mutual violation.

व्यतिरेकहेतु—a reason knwon to be concomitant by the process of violation only.

व्यवस्था—fixation, settlement.

व्यवहार—practice, use.

व्याप्यत्व—property of being less extensive, inclusiveness.

व्यापकत्व—property of being wider.

व्यभिचार—deviation.

मध्यस्थ—judge, one who is impartial.

मान—knowldege, means of knowldege.

योग्यता—compatibility, fitness.

लक्षण—definition, differentiating attribute.

लक्षणा—implication.

लाक्षणिक—secondary, implied.

लिङ्ग—mark, sign.

लिङ्गपरामर्श—synthetic consideration of the mark.

लिङ्गी—inferable property having a mark.

शाब्दज्ञान—verbal apprehension.

सपक्ष—similar instances.

समयबन्ध—bound by an agreement, taking of oath.

संशय—doubt.

सविकल्पकज्ञान—propositional awareness

सन्निकर्ष—sensory connection.

सम्प्रदाय—traditional school.

सादृश्य—similarity.

साधन—means to an end.

साध्य—inferable property.

सामान्य—genus, universal, general, common.

समान्यलक्षण—general attribute/definition, super-normal relation by generic attribute.

सिद्ध—accomplished, effected, acquired.

स्थापना—introduction, proposition, dialectical proof of a proposition.

स्वरूप—nature, peculiarity, character.

हेत्वाभास—feigned/counterfeited/simulating pseudo reason.

Bibliography

1. A Descriptive Catalogue of Sanskrit Manuscripts in the collection of Government Sanskrit College, Calcutta Vol. 1, Part-I, ed., B.M. Tarkavedantatirtha, Part II and III, ed. J.C. Tarktirtha, Government Sanskrit College, Calcutta 1963, 1965 and 1969.
2. A Descriptive Catalogue of the Sanskrit Manuscripts in the Government Collections of the Asiatic Society, Calcutta, vol. XI, ed. MM. Haraprasad Shastri, The Asiatic Society, Calcutta, 1957.
3. *Avayavaprakaraṇam* (Gādādharī), ed., Jwalaprasad Gauḍ Chowkhamba Sansrkit Series Office, Varanasi Kasi Sanskrit Series-202.
4. *Avayavacintāmaṇi of Gaṅgeśa with Māthurī and Jāgadīśī,* Ed. S.C. Goswami., 1st ed., Sanskrit Pustak Bhandar, Calcutta, 1991.
5. Apte, Vaman Shivram, *The Practical Sanskrit-English Dictionary,* Patna, 3rd edition, Motilal Banarsidass, Delhi, Varanasi, 1965.
6. Banerjee, Nandita, *The Concept of Logical Fallacies,* Sanskrit Pustak Bhandar, Calcutta, 1977.
7. Bhattacharya, D.C.:
   (a) *Baāge Navya Nyāya-Carcā* (in Bengali), Bangiya Sahitya Parishad, Calcutta, 1941.
   (b) *History of Navya-Nyāya in Mithila,* Mithila Institute, Darbhanga, 1958.
8. *Bhattacharya, Gopikamohan, Navya-Nyāya: Some Logical Problems in Historical Perspective,* Bharatiya Vidya Prakasan, New Delhi, 1978.
9. Bhattacharya, Sibjiban, *Gadādhara's Theory of Objective,* Part-I and II, ICPR, New Delhi, 1990 .
10. Bhattacharya, Tarasankar, *The Nature of Vyāpti,* Government Sanskrit College, Calcutta, 1970.
11. *Bhāṣāratnam* of Kaṇāda Tarkavāgiśa, ed. by MM. Kalipada

Tarkacharya, The Sanskrit Sahitya Parishat, Calcutta, 1936.

12. Catalogus Catalogorum, ed. Aufrecht, Theodor, vols. I and II, Indological Book House, Delhi, Varanasi, Reprint, 1989.
13. Chatterjee, S.C. *The Nyāya Theory of Knowledge,* University of Calcutta, 1978.
14. Das, Sunil Kumar, *The Nyāya Theory of Supernormal Perception,* Sanskrit Pustak Bhandar, Calcutta, 1988.
15. Encyclopaedia of Indian Philosophy, vols. I, II and VI, ed, Karl, H. Potter, Motilal Banarsidass, Delhi, 1983, 1983, 1995.
16. Gangopadhyaya, M.K., *Indian Logic and Its Sources: On Validity of Inference,* Munshiram Manoharlal, New Delhi, 1984.
17. Goswami, S.C.:
    (a) *Concept of Anuyogitā* (subjunctness) in Navya-Nyāya, Journal of the Dept. of Sanskrit, Rabindra Bharati University, vol. XIII, pp. 36-38.
    (b) *Editing of Nyāya-texts from Manuscript-sources,* JDS, RBU, vol. VIII, pp. 65-77.
    (c) *Interpretation of Nyāyāvayava* and Kaṇāda Tarkavāgiśa, Rabindra Bharati Patrika (2005), vol. XIV pp. 163-66.
    (d) *Mechanism of De-limiting Attribute (Avacchedaka) in Navya-Nyāya,* JDS. RBU, vol. X, pp. 19-32.
    (e) *The Concept of Pratiyogitā in Navya-Nyāya,* Sanskritic Studies: Modern Sensibilities (2004), Academic Staff College and Dept. of Sanskrit, University of Calcutta, pp. 58-65.
18. Grimes John, *A Concise Dictionary of Indian Philosophy,* Madras University, 1988.
19. Guha, D. C., *Navya-Nyāya System of Logic,* Motilal Banarasidass, Delhi, Varanasi, rev. edition, 1979.
20. Gupta, Sarita, *Problem of Relations in Indian Philosophy,* Eastern Book Linkers, Delhi, 1984.
21. Hota, Kashinath and Mishra Arun Rajan, *Bibliography of Nyāya-Vaiśeṣika,* CASS, University of Poona, 1993.
22. Ingalls, D. H. H., *Materials for the Study of Navya-Nyāya-Logic,* Motilal Banarsidass, Delhi, Varanasi, 1988.
23. Jhalkikar, Bhimacharya, *Nyāyakoṣa or Dictionary of Technical Terms of Indian Philosophy,* The Bhandarkar Oriental Research Institute, Poona, 1978.
24. Katre, S. M., *Introduction to Indian Textual Criticism,* Karnatak Publishing House, Bombay, 1941.
25. Misra, Umesh, *History of Indian Philosophy,* vol. II, Allahabad: Tirabhukti Publication, 1966.

26. Mohanty, J.N., *Gaṅgeśa's Theory of Truth*, Motilal Banarsidass, Delhi, 1989.
27. Monier Williams, Sir M., *A Sanskrit-English Dictionary*, Motilal Banarsidass, Delhi, nineth reprint, 1984.
28. Motilal. B. K.:
    (a) *The Navya-Nyāya Doctrine of Negation*, Harvard University Press, 1968.
    (b) *A History of Indian Literature* (*Nyāya-Vaiśeṣika*), J. Gonda. Series, Otto Harrassowitz, Wiesbaden, Germany, 1977.
29. Mukhopadhyaya, Bijoy Nath, *Administration of Manuscript Libraries with Special Reference to Sanskrit Manuscripts*, Government Sanskrit College Research Series No. CXXVIII, Calcutta, 1985.
30. Murty, R.S. Shivaganesha, *Introduction to Manuscriptology*, Sharada Publishing House, Delhi, 1996.
31. New Catalogus Catalogorum, vol. I (rev. ed), II, and III , ed., Dr. V. Raghavan, University of Madras, 1966, 1967, 1968.
32. Nyāyaratna, MM. Mahesh Chandra, *Navya-Nyāya Bhāṣāpradpa*, Government Sanskrit College, Calcutta, 1973.
33. *Nyāyatātparyadīpikā* of Bhaṭṭavāgīśvara, ed., Kishorenath Jha, Ganganatha Jha Kendriya Vidyapeetha, Allahabad, 1979.
34. Saha, Sukharanjan, *Perspectives on Nyāya-Logic and Epistemology*, K.P. Bagchi and Co., Calcutta, 1987.
35. *Studies in History of Indian Philosophy*, ed., Chattopadhyaya, Deviprasad, vols. I, II and III, K.P. Bagchi, Calcutta, reprint, 1990.
36. *Tattvacintāmaṇi-Gādādharī*, vol. I (Anumāna), ed., Kirtyananda Jha, Chowkhamba, Varanasi, 1970.
37. *Tattvacintāmaṇiprakāśa* of Rucidutta, vol. II, ed., M.S. Ramanuja Tatacarya, Samskrita Vidyapeetha, Tirupati, 1973.
38. *Tattvacintāmaṇi* with *Māthurī*, ed., Kamakhyanatha Sanskrit Tarkavagiĺa, vol. II, parts I and II, Chowkhamba Pratisthan, 1990.
39. Tarkatirtha, Pt. Dayal Krishna, *Anumānacintāmaṇi* (Bengali), Kadipur, P.O. Balagunj, Dist. Srihatta, BS, 1332.
40. Tarkatirtha, Srimohan and Bhattacharya, D.C., *Bhāratīya Darśana-koṣa* (Bengali), Government Sanskrit College, Calcutta, 1978.
41. Tarkavāgiśa, MM. Phanibhusana, *Nyāyaparicaya*, Paschim-banga Rajya, Pustak Parsad, Calcutta, second edition, 1986.
42. Vidyabhusan, S.C., *History of Indian Logic*, Motilal Banarsidass, Delhi, reprint 1971.

43. *Viṣayatāvādaḥ* of Harirama, ed., V.N. Jha, University of Poona, 1987.

44. *Vyāptipañcak* (with Bengali exposition), ed. Rajendranath Ghosh, Paschim Banga Pustak Parsad, Calcutta, rev. ed., 1982.

45. *Kaṇādaṭippaṇī* (A commentary on Gaṅgeśa's Avayavacintāmaṇi), ed., S.C. Goswami, Rabindra Bharati University, Kolkata, March, 2006.

46. Maitra, Sushil Kumar, *Fundamental Questions of Indian Metaphysics and Logic,* University of Calcutta, 1974.